LETTERS OF GRACE

Vol. 1 - He is...

AARON KINCAID

Aaron Kincaid
Letters of Grace: Vol. 1 - He is...

Cover Artwork by Jaiden Kincaid

Published by BooxAi
ISBN: 978-965-578-916-4

Grace has exerted Himself through Pastor Aaron and continues to do so. This book will not be in lack of that same power.

Pastor Kyle Brady,
Pastor of Juneau Revival Center

I have watched Pastor Aaron and Cyndi Kincaid follow their passion for many years. Their passion and calling, is to see people find new freedom from bondage. Letters of Grace will build your faith to new levels. When you read the accounts of people who had given up on life only to find the Gospel of Grace through miracles of healing. I recommend you keep a copy of this book close by to reread everytime you find yourself facing in crisis.

Kerry Kirkwood,
Pastor and Author
Trinity Fellowship

Pastor Aaron Kincaid has truly captivated us with his profound exploration of the topic of grace in his latest book, "Letters of Grace." It becomes evident that Pastor Aaron is not just an author; he's a vessel touched by God's grace, driven by a genuine passion to help others comprehend the fullness of God's grace.

In this thought-provoking work, Pastor Aaron addresses prevalent misconceptions about grace that have been recycled by various authors and pastors over the past few decades. He challenges readers to view grace through the lens of God's unconditional love for both the church and the sinner.

One of the book's highlights is Pastor Aaron's courage to delve into scriptures that are often misunderstood or taken for granted in discussions about grace. He skillfully unpacks deeper meanings, providing readers with a richer understanding of grace from a biblical perspective.

"Letters of Grace" is not merely a theological discourse; it weaves in personal narratives of remarkable healings and instances where God's presence manifested in daily lives. These stories serve not only to inspire but to fortify the reader's faith.

The book also features insightful exegesis of biblical stories, with a particular focus on Jesus and His boundless love, grace, and mercy. The sections devoted to these themes are undoubtedly the book's crowning jewels.

In essence, "Letters of Grace" is a source of inspiration, a builder of faith, and an expansive guide to understanding the diverse ways in which God can work through individuals, as vividly portrayed in the stories within. I wholeheartedly recommend adding this transformative work to your reading list—it's a journey worth undertaking.

Thomas McDaniels
Pastor/Author/Public Speaker/Life Coach
Founder of Lifebridge Christian Center
Thomas McDaniels Ministries
Network 411 Ministries

Contents

I would like to dedicate this book to my wife Cyndi, who for the last 30 years has been by my side. Through all of life's twists and turns, has consistently said "Let's just trust the Lord!".

Cyndi, I love you beyond words! Thank you for taking the journey with me always and pointing me to Jesus in the journey. You are the love of my life, my best friend, and an amazing mother to our children.

"She carefully watches everything in her household and suffers nothing from laziness. Her children stand and bless her. Her husband praises her: "There are many virtuous and capable women in the world, but you surpass them all!"

Proverbs 31:27-29 NLT

Prologue

"Hey!! It's me! Look at this!! I haven't been able to stand up straight like this in six or seven years!" The look on her face I will never forget. She then proudly exclaimed, "Oh and I ate enchiladas last night with no problems!"

We hadn't seen April in 5 days. It was July 4th and the whole town was out in the clearing near the ocean inlet surrounded by beautiful white-capped mountains. It was a scene straight out of a Hallmark movie. We had met April in a little shop just five days earlier. She had seen our team praying for a friend of hers. When we finished praying we walked into the little corner shop and April came walking into sight behind her counter. She immediately asked to talk to us. As we stood there at the counter she asked if we could pray with her as well. She believed the Lord could heal her. I had observed when she first walked out that she was bent over somewhat and walked with a slight limp. She told us that she was a believer in Jesus and that she knew she could receive her healing from the scoliosis she had been born with, and now had her crippled over. Her being a woman, and my wife and another lady standing closer to her, I stepped back just a bit and allowed the ladies to pray with her while I prayed as well thanking Jesus for healing her body.

As it wrapped up I stepped back up closer and the other lady with my wife, our friend Amy received a word from the Lord concerning April's stomach. Amy immediately said, "And whatever is going in with your stomach Jesus is healing it right now as well!" April said, "Thank you, Jesus!" She then told us how she had had an issue the previous year with her stomach and almost died. She told us how she was on a very specific diet of small and bland foods, but again received her healing! Now here it was five days later on a beautiful Alaskan day in the middle of hundreds of people at the town picnic. We had just arrived back from a different town 6 hours away, and she found us in the crowd! Shows herself to us and gives Jesus the praise!

While there is a little more to that story of April, I will never forget that moment in time. That day while it's hard to describe in words, I will just say for me it was almost like a "yes this is real" moment between me and Jesus. The Lord had been doing a lot in our lives in ministry for the last six years. After leaving a great career in law enforcement to follow the leading of the Lord, my wife Cyndi and our three children Jaiden, Levi, and Kynzie, packed up our house and moved to the little town of Winona, Texas. It was just up the road a few minutes in the town of Gladewater we founded a ministry called Restored180 for women coming off drugs and alcohol. How the Lord dropped the facility in our laps is a testimony for another time. That said, the doors to Restored180 opened on November 20, 2017, full throttle!

Over the next almost six years we ministered to

hundreds of women from all over. In the midst of that, in 2019, we started a church ministry called *Life180* Church. Our vision was simple, build the church! Notice I didn't say build *a* church. We wanted to minister to the broken, and we also knew that there were a lot of broken in the church! With the women's ministry running full and the church ministry growing, 2020 came and like many Covid hit, we saw some losses. Also like many, I struggled with the "long-haulers" post Covid symptoms. After 9 months of recovery, things just didn't seem like they were the same. I began asking the Lord what was wrong. Why does it seem as though we have lost our drive? Where was the passion? Sure we were exhausted, and sure we had worked for years 80-100 hours a week. But we were seeing lives changed! We were doing what the Lord called us to do! But no matter how much we tried to just resume what had been, Cyndi and I both knew it. There was a shift coming! Something was going to change. When the shift would happen we were not sure, so we would stay faithful to what was in front of us until the Lord revealed it to us.

In January of 2023 as I was praying one day I heard the Lord say "This will be a year of expansion." That's it! I was thrilled. I thought to myself "Okay the ministry is going to expand!" That ranch property is finally going to happen! We will be able to open a men's restoration center and grow the women's ministry! We will have a church building of our own! I was very satisfied and thought I should be looking towards properties and began praying that way as well.

A couple of months later, in one week we received two prophetic words from very trusted sources. People we know without a doubt hear from the Lord. Both told us that the buildings were on the way. We said thank you, Jesus!

Now June of 2023 had arrived and for almost 8 weeks prior we had been seeing more and more signs, wonders, and miracles in our church meetings. A lady with a lung condition healed. The doctor took her off the oxygen tank and said her lungs were great. A couple of people were delivered from demonic possession and many more set free from demonic oppression. Another lady healed of cancer. Cyndi and I knew the Lord was up to something. We invited a lady we knew of through a mutual friend, to come and minister. Her name is Amy Kemp and she started a ministry years ago called Recipients of Grace. We knew she ministered in Denmark a lot and the Lord was using her to preach the gospel. We also knew there had been many healed and set free in her meetings. Amy came and it was a great night with Jesus. Several people were healed and set free. After everyone had left, we had finished cleaning up and my wife and I were talking with Amy and a friend she had brought with her. A couple of other folks were still hanging around as well. My wife Cyndi brought up the idea that Amy and her team should pray about going to Alaska one day to minister.

Suddenly the Holy Spirit's tangible presence showed up in the midst of us.

His presence was so strong, that my wife collapsed to the floor (something she does not normally do) and I found myself leaning against a wall. Amy and her friend both looked big-eyed and smiled a little unsteady on their feet as well. I remember saying at that moment, "Ok, wow. What is happening right now?". Amy said, "Y'all know what this means right? We're all going to Alaska". We all agreed that the Lord had just put His hand on us at that moment and assigned us to go. We all spent days talking to the Lord about the details of the trip. We came to agree on 10 days and we would all trust the Lord to provide whatever we needed financially for the trip. Within a week the finances came in to purchase the airline tickets. As we shared about the ministry trip with others, more finances came in and we knew it was just confirmation from Jesus. On the day we were leaving for Alaska, just a couple of weeks later, I asked the Lord why we were going to Alaska. I heard the Lord say "I am taking you on a show and tell journey. I am going to show you things and then tell you things." This book is the result of the revelation the Lord gave me and my wife Cyndi and while on the journey and even more after we came back home.

My wife and I have preached in numerous places. Over the years I have ministered in countries around the world. We have preached the unconditional Love of Jesus through His Word and the presence of the Holy Spirit to change lives for over 25 years. Seeing fruit here and there, always believing we were at least planting seeds and that we may never know the fruit of our labor. Never did we ever think that some of what we preached, those little Christian sayings we had learned growing up in church and ministry were the reason why we didn't see consistent miracles. Don't get me wrong, we saw lives touched by Jesus and we saw people changed by the power of His love. And we saw some miracles when people received in faith. We saw more than some ministers we had talked to over the years. Watching the Spirit of God transform the lives of the women who came through our Restored180 program grew our faith in a lot of ways! We saw so many lives changed for the glory of God in the past six years. But when something didn't go right we would wonder what we did wrong. But as it turned out 2023 was a year of expansion. We just didn't know what the Lord had in store and that the expansion included expanding our understanding of His new covenant and our sphere of influence in the Kingdom. I hope this book will bring that same revelation to you and that you are empowered and set free just like we were to preach the gospel of Grace.

"And he said to them, “This is my blood of the new covenant, which is poured out for many."

Mark 14:24

For sin will have no dominion over you, since you are not under law but under grace.

Romans 6:14 ESV

ONE

It must be right

"IT JUST DOESN'T MAKE sense! I have read it over and over. The Bible, it just doesn't make sense!"

So what about the preacher? "Preach that!"

"Amen pastor", then look at a friend, "I don't get what he means", or "Man, this guy!"

"I mean it must be right because the pastor said it!"

You see, I grew up in church. I had the Ten Commandments memorized by the time I was in third grade. We sang them as a song at church to help us kids remember how not to make God mad at us. I remember my mom put me on the Bible trivia team in fourth grade. I memorized so much scripture just from the trivia practice cards. I was pretty good at trivia too. I had no idea what they meant but I could fill in the blank or finish the sentence, even tell you the reference in the Bible where the scripture was found. So years later when I moved in with my dad, going to church was just part of life. Only now I began to attend my dad's church. These people were wild. They fell down when the pastor prayed for them, and sang for almost two hours. I saw my dad singing and lifting his hands, a lot like the church my mom attended when I was younger. So at 12 years old I just thought well my dad does it, and everyone else is doing it, I better get to it if I want to be closer to God and as spiritual as them.

So I began to raise my hands. I didn't get why, but it was a learned behavior at that point in my life, and not in response to the love of God. I went to a private Christian school for a while. I learned more about the Bible and God and how to be more spiritual. But as I grew into my older teen years, I still didn't understand the Bible. I went to church all the time. I just went along with whatever the pastor said was the right way to live for God because the pastor was "the man of God". I even sang on the worship team and learned to play drums and bass. I was a leader in my youth church. Prayed for people and sometimes saw the miraculous. I am sure that I am not the only one who has come across this issue as a Christian. In fact, at almost every meeting I have preached in the last six months, I have asked this question to the people and I have never had less than half of the people raise their hands in agreement that they too, have experienced this lack of understanding. We just always assumed since the person speaking is using the Bible and they are the one in "ministry", it must be right.

The one thing that was real to me and that I did understand pretty well was that God was real, and in the midst of chaotic family drama, I could feel His peace and presence. I didn't understand His Bible really and would fall asleep trying to read it because that's what good Christians do. "If you're not in your Word, you won't make it in this world, because if you want to show God you are serious and you want Him to bless your life, you better **show** Him you're serious," or "If you don't have a prayer life, you will never get right with God or walk in victory!"

Man, in my church if you didn't show up to 5:42 am prayer, you weren't spiritual and you probably weren't even a real believer. Unless you were at work of course. Then you better be paying that tithe to "God's house". So I would drag myself to prayer at 5:42 am once a week or every other week just to show everyone I was serious about being spiritual for God. And I made sure to give my ten percent off the gross wages amount of my paycheck. When the pastor got up and read God's word that said something about robbing God and I would be cursed, I wasn't stupid and I made sure that wasn't going to happen to me. I would also attend a youth prayer meeting on Friday nights. It was different in a lot of ways, mainly I could feel the presence of God, His Holy Spirit, as we prayed without stopping for hours. Many prayed in the Spirit in a heavenly language, which I received as a gift from the Lord one afternoon as well. So there was all this teaching, and preaching that I didn't get half of, but then there were encounters with Jesus through His Holy Spirit that showed me how real God was in my life. We serve a real God who sent His Holy Spirit to this earth to lead us and guide us into all Truth. It has been a long journey of figuring out what He was teaching me along the way. There was so much I just couldn't understand about His Word, and that made it difficult to understand what He was trying to teach me. He has been so patient with me and I am still learning from Him today. How about you, friend?

I'm sure many of you can relate in one way or another. So many have told me they do, especially when it comes to truly understanding the Bible when it is being taught or preached. Others try to read the Bible for themselves and just don't get it. If you were like me, raised in church, and taught the Bible, memorizing scripture even, and you're not sure why God did this or that, or said this or that, you are not alone. Maybe you didn't grow up in church, and you are new to trying to figure out the life of a believer or just somewhere between one and the other. This short book is for you, to get you started on this life journey with Jesus and give you some Truth about the Word of God that will help you to understand God's word and rightly believe. It's only when we have right believing, that living how Jesus intended is produced in our lives. As we go, of course, I will bring the scripture into the reading as well. For instance, there is a reason we found it hard, and many still do, to understand the Word of Truth. The Bible specifically tells us the reason! In 2 Corinthians 3. Let's look at that now!

> "But the people's minds were hardened, and **to this day** whenever the old covenant is being read, the same veil covers their minds **so they cannot understand the truth.** And this veil can be removed only by believing in Christ. **Yes, even today** when they read Moses' writings, **their hearts are covered with that veil, and they do not understand."**
>
> 2 Corinthians 3:14-15 NLT

Do you see that my friend? To this day, the Bible says that when the old covenant is preached, a veil covers the people's minds and hearts and they cannot understand the Truth. It wasn't our fault. The problem is we have so many in the church today teaching the old covenant of law and a mixture of the old covenant of law with the new covenant of Grace and people just do not understand it. Keep in mind that I am not saying that people are ignorant of the Word. I am not saying they don't know the Bible. I am saying many, like me back then, can probably quote the scriptures, but cannot understand Grace and Truth. Jesus came as Grace and Truth to enact a new covenant that would redeem people back to the Father. But if I ask the average church-going believer what the new covenant of His blood is, or what the gospel of Grace is, few seem to understand what I am asking, let alone the ability to articulate what it is that Jesus established for us. If you ask a Christian why Jesus died on the cross, they will tell you for our sins so we can go to heaven when we die! You might get a few more to say that "by His stripes, we are healed" but can't explain how to receive the freegift of healing that those stripes purchased for us. All of this is because there is so much law and Grace mixed in our preaching today and has been for so many years. Doctrines are built on it! Denominations have been established on it. And it doesn't matter how much of one or the other you lean towards. When Paul said in Galatians 5, "A little leaven leavens the whole lump," (Galatians 5:9 ESV) that's what he is saying. Even a little bit of the old covenant of law or its ways, when mixed in with the new covenant of Grace that Jesus established by His blood, ruins it for everyone who hears because that little bit brings a veil.

He is talking to the believers in Galatia who had already received the Truth of Jesus, the gospel of Grace, and His new covenant. The problem came when some of the local Pharisees came into the church of Galatia and told them they had to keep the law of the old covenant as well.

Suddenly there was sin and other problems and Paul asked them, "Who bewitched you"?

Jesus warned us of this when He told the Pharisees that you cannot put new wine in old wineskins. Many charismatics have taught us for years that the new wine was a new or fresh outpouring of the Holy Spirit and then told us we needed to get right with God to become the new wineskin because the old wineskin would rupture and that would ruin the old wineskin and the new wine, both. Does that make sense to you?

Let's break this down for a minute: So what you are saying is that I am an old wineskin and that if I don't get right and become the new wineskin, the Holy Spirit's outpouring of Himself when it gets to me will rupture me and ruin me, and the Spirit of God? Does that make any sense at all? Especially when we see Jesus talking to the Pharisees when He is comparing the old way to the new way He had come to establish. No, it doesn't make sense at all. So many of us spent time begging God to forgive us of our sins from a place of condemnation just so we wouldn't miss the outpouring of the Holy Spirit. Then after the revival was over, so many of us just kept walking in condemnation and guilt and shame, because when we got home and the memories, feelings, and thoughts just came right back, it was like, "Well that was fun!" I can't wait until I can get back to the next meeting so I can get more of the Holy Spirit poured into me. Which is just a form of emotionalism in response to His manifested presence. But until then we continued to contend with condemnation because we never left practicing the old ways even though Jesus brought a new way.

So when we see the comparison is really about two

covenants, the old law and its ways and the new covenant of Grace, and that you can't mix them or the "whole batch is ruined" or if you try to put the new covenant of Grace into the old covenant of law, it will rupture the old and ruin them both for us. Then you can begin to see that when we preach the gospel to people, and if we want to receive all that Jesus died for, all the promises that the finished work of the cross established for us, if we want to make disciples of all nations, if we want to see faith come to people, then when we preach the gospel **it must be right**!

Have you ever seen someone set free when the Ten Commandments are preached? It doesn't have to be a lot, we don't have to know the whole Bible, Paul said to live up to what we have already learned, but we need to get this right because the gospel is the power of God for salvation. We must rightly divide the Word of Truth! This is what Paul is talking about in 2 Timothy 2. We don't have to be ashamed when we study the Word of Truth, and we know it and understand it, then we will be free from shame (the law of condemnation) because we know we are rightly presenting the Word of Truth. So the next time you listen to the preacher or turn on that podcast, ask Jesus to reveal law and Grace, and no I won't apologize for introducing this to you. I know I am not alone when I say I am sick and tired of seeing and meeting believers in Jesus who live every day with guilt and shame, condemnation and fear, because of what they were taught.

TWO

The revealing

IT WAS early June of 2023, on a Friday night at one of our *Life180* meetings. My wife and I founded *Life180* in 2019 with the mandate to build up the church, the body of Christ. Not to build a church, but the Church. The meetings are on Friday nights and the Lord shows up so strongly. The Spirit of God has been transforming lives through these meetings.

After four years, we were seeing a stronger move of the Lord. A lady was healed of cancer, and then another lady's lungs were healed after Covid had wrecked her body. Then a woman who had been sexually traumatized as a child was healed and set free. Then a man's back pain was healed, another man's knee was healed, then a woman was set free and several demons cast out of her. Of course, we were excited about what the Lord was doing. We thought okay we must be doing something right finally. We had prayed and told the Lord we just wanted whatever He wanted.

It was now June of 2023 and we had invited a woman to come to minister. We had heard of her through a mutual friend and my wife Cyndi reached out to her one morning while praying over her and sent her a message the Lord gave her. That led to a conversation and an invitation. Ha! The Lord was up to something and we didn't have a clue at that time. But this Friday night in June, Amy Kemp came and ministered at our *Life180* meeting. The Lord moved powerfully and many were healed and set free.

The crazy part for us didn't happen until everyone had left except for a few of us: Amy and a friend that came with her, my wife Cyndi and myself, and a couple of others were standing around talking about Jesus and my wife brought up Alaska and that Amy and her team should pray about going and doing some ministry there. We had been there the year before on vacation and saw firsthand how oppressed a lot of the people there were, and heard how so many struggled with alcoholism and abuse. But back in that little church, in that moment something happened to us all.

It's hard to really explain, so I will just simply say it like this: Immediately after my wife said what she said about Alaska, there was an intense wave of the presence of God that fell on us all. In shock we were looking around at each other as the glory of God just became so heavy that my wife was now on the floor and I was leaning on a wall. We all just looked at each other. Amy said smiling, "Y'all know what this means right?" We were going to Alaska!

To say this was a challenge would be a little bit of an understatement. While I have traveled the world somewhat in my younger years, my wife Cyndi has only left our home state of Texas a few times in her lifetime. So to spontaneously say yes to the Lord's sending us 4000 miles from home, with no church contacts, missionary advisors, or ministry relationships. With a team of people we didn't know except by word of mouth and a short time of ministry, with no agenda other than follow the Holy Spirit as He directs us, I took it as more confirmation that my wife was so immediately for us going.

We said a simple prayer before leaving the church that night and told the Lord He had our yes and that we knew He would supply all the needs financially for the trip. He did just that within a couple of weeks. We had airline tickets and money for a rental car. On the flight there more money came in that would help cover food and lodging. We had prayed before leaving and all had peace that the Lord was speaking 10 days for this trip. And we went trusting Him for all provision. We had been there several days and the Lord had already healed people He brought into our path. I will get into the details more in the next "Letters of Grace", Vol. II.

That said, what I do want to share is the day we left, I prayed and asked the Lord why He was sending us to Alaska. I heard clearly in my spirit the Lord say, "I am taking you on a show and tell. I am going to show you, and then I am going to tell you." The showing part happened all along the trip. The craziest stuff, stuff people would probably not believe if I didn't have video evidence. Like a duck flying into our driving lane causing me to slow down. Then as soon as I got closer the duck began to fly alongside my driver-side window looking at me. We made eye contact right before he flew back in front of our vehicle and stayed flying in our lane keeping me from driving more than 30 miles per hour for 3 minutes.

3 minutes. Have you ever seen a duck fly in a traffic lane perfectly for 3 minutes? Then as suddenly as he appeared he banked out to the right and flew out of sight. We all knew this was not normal and that the Lord put that duck in our lane for a reason. I will tell you later why I believe the Lord

did that. So the show part continued at places we stopped and shops we went into. A lady in unexplainable pain throughout her body, who had tried doctors and specialists, to know avail, was healed completely by Jesus in an instant when we prayed for her. Of course, the show part was fun and a huge joy to be a part of. But the telling part, almost all of it happened inside the vehicle. As I listened to this odd team of ladies share their experiences with Jesus, we talked about the Bible and scripture after scripture. We agreed on everything from a biblical stand point, but there was a revelation the Lord gave me through those conversations. In particular, with our friend Amy Kemp.

Amy would throw out the word Grace a lot. I began to think she was one of those grace doctrine people, but she didn't teach like them. So I finally asked her if she believed in the grace doctrine. She said she believed in the gospel of Grace. As we talked I explained to her that I believed the word of God and I think we are on the same page, but I have just always stayed away from the "grace doctrine" because every time I had heard it taught, it led to compromise. People would tell me their sin was okay to keep living in because they were “under grace”. I knew even as a younger youth pastor that scripturally that was wrong. The Bible specifically says it is not an excuse to keep on living in sin. And that's when the Lord spoke to my heart through Amy as we were driving down the road. Seeing signs, wonders, and miracles happen almost every time we stopped and got out of the car, here in the car the Lord was using this little Jesus preaching woman, to speak revelation to me. She said, “That's not Grace, Grace is not a doctrine or thing. Grace is a person, the person of Jesus Christ!" With this confident smile on her face, it hit me like a light that just suddenly came on brighter than the other lights, and all I could say was, "That makes a lot more sense!"

The truth was I felt like my hands were suddenly untied and knew the Lord was indeed teaching, telling me His story through the ten days of talking and listening to this woman. The Lord sent us far away from everything else in life, so He would have our undivided attention. Throughout the trip, Cyndi and I would talk in our hotel rooms about this, and how we both felt like we had this head knowledge of the information, but somehow we just weren't applying it or just didn't understand it the way we were meant to. And now after 25-plus years of ministry, we feel like Jesus took us on a special trip just to teach us and show us how the Gospel of Grace, the good news of Jesus truly is the power of God that leads to salvation in Jesus. How the kingdom of God because of Jesus' blood and the finished work of the cross is all about receiving, not achieving. That Jesus is Grace! The Bible says in John 1 that the law was given, but Grace and Truth came. It's crazy you might say, but since then, the Bible has made perfect sense! More than that, things connect and it's easy to rightly divide the Word. To put law where God put it, away! Replacing it with a new covenant of Grace in Jesus.

THREE

The person... Grace

As I SAT TALKING to the Lord about how to show everyone I could that He is Grace. Jesus is the person of Grace and Truth, He reminded me that God is Love. Love is a person! He reminded me that He is the Way, the Truth, and the Life. These are the person of Jesus Christ. And all those pronouns, are the embodiment of Jesus. So that is why they are only found **in Christ!**

So then as we look at scripture that speaks of Grace, we can use His name Jesus, or the character, descriptor, or adjective of Him in the same place. You know what? It works! Let me show you some examples:

> "God saved you by his grace (*Son Jesus - John 3:16*) when you believed. And you can't take credit for this; it is a gift from God. Salvation is not a reward for the good things we have done, so none of us can boast about it. For we are God's masterpiece. He has created us anew in

> Christ Jesus, so we can do the good things he planned for us long ago."
>
> Ephesians 2:8-10 NLT

Because Jesus was unmerited, unearned, and underserved. And because He loves, blesses, saves, heals, and restores, not because of what we do, but simply because of who He is, He is the person of Grace:

> "Each time he said, "My grace (Jesus) is all you need. My power works best in weakness." So now I am glad to boast about my weaknesses so that the power of Christ can work through me."
>
> 2 Corinthians 12:9 NLT

Again, we see Jesus is the Grace, just like He is the Way, the Truth, the Life, the Word and He is Love! As we begin to see Him and all that He is, and then we begin to believe that He is in us, it is no wonder the Bible says "we have this treasure in jars of clay!" (2 Corinthians 4:7) It's no wonder that the Bible says, "Greater is He that is in us than he that is in this world!" (1 John 4:4). The believers, adopted and grafted in, now sons and daughters of our Father God through Christ (Romans 8:15). We begin to see the vastness, "how deep and how wide..." (Ephesians 3:18-19) is the love of Christ, that He would come as a new covenant of Grace and Himself come as the Truth, all that Jesus accomplished on the cross. He is the very person of Grace, Truth, Hope, Love, Redeemer, and King. And so much more! Our Healer, Restorer, Provider, and the Author and Perfector of our

Faith. Jesus is our Grace and Truth that came in the flesh to bring a new life to us and He is all that the covenant of His blood entails. So as we fix our eyes on Jesus, we become all that He purposed us to be, in Him. He did the work and He does the work in us.

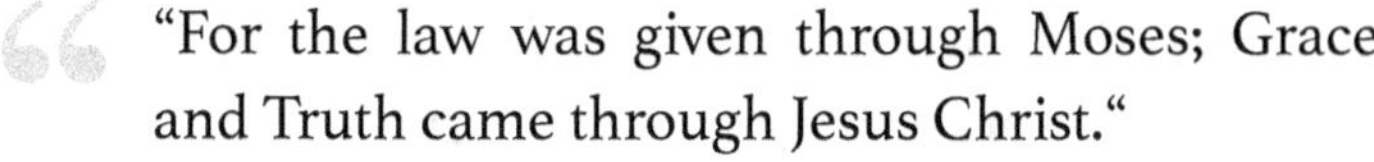

> "For the law was given through Moses; Grace and Truth came through Jesus Christ."
>
> John 1:17 ESV

Grace and Truth came in person. Jesus is that Grace and Truth. When we begin to see that Jesus is the new covenant, we understand why He said He is the Way, the Truth, and the Life. We can live in Him and He through us in the beautiful covenant of Grace. Grace is good news because the gospel is not just that Jesus came, was born, lived a sin-free life, and died on the cross for our sins. He is so much more! He came so that we could be as He is now, by surrendering to Grace. Jesus our Grace and Truth came so that we could be redeemed back to the Father as sons and daughters, so that we become one with Jesus and the Father just as Jesus prayed in John 17.

> "When Jesus had spoken these words, he lifted his eyes to heaven, and said, 'Father, the hour has come; glorify your Son that the Son may glorify you, since you have given him authority over all flesh, to give eternal life to all whom you have given him. And this is eternal life, that they know you, the only true God, and Jesus Christ whom you have sent. I glorified you on earth,

having accomplished the work that you gave me to do. And now, Father, glorify me in your own presence with the glory that I had with you before the world existed. I have manifested your name to the people whom you gave me out of the world. Yours they were, and you gave them to me, and they have kept your word. Now they know that everything that you have given me is from you. For I have given them the words that you gave me, and they have received them and have come to know in truth that I came from you; and they have believed that you sent me. I am praying for them. I am not praying for the world but for those whom you have given me, for they are yours. All mine are yours, and yours are mine, and I am glorified in them. And I am no longer in the world, but they are in the world, and I am coming to you. Holy Father, keep them in your name, which you have given me, that they may be one, even as we are one. While I was with them, I kept them in your name, which you have given me. I have guarded them, and not one of them has been lost except the son of destruction, that the Scripture might be fulfilled. But now I am coming to you, and these things I speak in the world, that they may have my joy fulfilled in themselves. I have given them your word, and the world has hated them because they are not of the world, just as I am not of the world. I do not ask that you take them out of the world, but that you keep them from the evil one. They are not of the world, just as I am not of the world. Sanctify them in the truth; your word is truth. As you sent me into the world, so I have sent them into the world. And for their sake, I consecrate myself, that they also may be sanctified in truth. "I do not ask for these only, but also for those who will believe in me through their word, **that they may all be one, just as you, Father, are in me, and I in you, that they also may be in us, so that the world may believe that you have sent me. The glory that you have given me I have given to them, that they may be one even as we are one, I in them and you in me, that they may become perfectly one, so that the world may know that you sent me and loved them even as you loved me.** Father, I desire that they also, whom you have given me, may be with me where I am, to see my glory that you have given me because you loved me before the foundation of the world. O righteous Father, even though the world does not know you, I know you, and these know that you have sent me. I made known to them your name, and I will continue to make it known, that the love with which you have loved me may be in them, and I in them."

John 17:1-26 ESV

This is a very revealing conversation that Jesus had with the Father. Jesus is expressing His desire to the Father that just as He and the Father are One, and we too would be as one, with He and the Father. You might say "well pastor when we die we will go and be with Jesus and the Father and that's when we will finally be one with them". While that is true concerning what will happen when we step into eternity to be with Jesus, Jesus told us that He would send the Promised One, the Holy Spirit. The Holy Spirit is the literal Spirit of God, and the Spirit of Jesus that lives in us, making us one with the Father and Jesus through His Spirit. (John 14:16-20) This is more scriptural evidence that backs up what John later says in his letter to the believers declaring that "as He is, so are we in the earth" speaking of Jesus. When we put the Truth that Jesus is Grace together with the Truth that He is one with us, living in us through His Holy Spirit, then that begins to pull into alignment with a lot of other scriptures concerning what our lives should be in Christ. It's no wonder Jesus said to go into all the world and preach the gospel! When we go where He leads us by His Spirit, it is His purpose and plan to reach others. He reveals Himself through the surrendered in Him. He speaks through us, to tell others the Truth so they will receive Him and be born again. When we understand that this work is not of our doing, but by His leading, we see why God said in the scripture in Zechariah 4:6 "...not by might, nor by power, but by my Spirit says the Lord." Then Paul writes in 1 Corinthians 3 that he didn't bring a message that was of men's wisdom, but that he came in demonstration of the Spirit of God and of power so that our faith would not rest in men or women, but in God. It further brings together that we are "His masterpiece", that we are "a light", a "city on a hill", that we are "vessels of honor ready for the masters use", and even more a substantiated knowing that "greater works than these will you do" as Jesus told us.

What I am trying to drive home here is this. When we

have the right thinking, knowing, and believing, when we understand that Grace and Truth came to us according to the Word of God, then we can receive the revelation of who we truly are supposed to be in Jesus. More importantly, it's not just who we are supposed to be, but that we are all that He is because He is in us. So we became the message of Grace and Truth to the world. Our lives are to reveal the glory of Jesus in us. This is Him in us. The beautiful exchange is that we don't have to make any effort to be who Jesus has made us. We only have to surrender our life to Him. He is Grace, so in our surrender, He does it all. Our part is to stare at Jesus all day long, fix our thoughts on things of Him, and listen to His voice. Well, that sounds real spiritual pastor, but I work at a business where if I don't focus and do my job right bad things can happen and I could lose my job.

Can you imagine, Jesus doing your job through you? Imagine doing your job with such Grace, that others would say of you, there is something different about that person. Imagine co-workers asking, "how do you make it look so easy?" Or "how do you stay so calm when everyone else is stressed out?" You see Jesus gave you that job in the first place. He put you there on an assignment from heaven. He will do the work through you and bless you, favor you, and use you as a light if you allow Him to live through you. So many of us, separate our jobs from our life in Jesus. For whatever reason, but a lot of times it is because of the fear of being fired or making a co-worker mad. Maybe it's not a fear of losing your job, but an insecurity that you could be used by the Lord. When we see life like this, our jobs or school, whatever it is, we are seeing through our natural eyes and leaning on "our own understanding." But when we believe that Jesus wants to live through us and that we can trust in Him as our everything, then that faith in Him removes the fear of man. It removes the "what ifs" because our eyes are locked on Jesus and we are listening to His voice. We know that in obeying His voice, He knows what He is doing. If man rejects us they are not rejecting us, they are rejecting the One that sent us. If they make fun of us or fire us, Jesus already knew that was coming, and He has already prepared our next assignment. We just keep following Him and the provision comes through Him and all that we need. It's not just about our job or provision, it's about our entire lives. It's how we talk to others, how we respond to others, it's about allowing Jesus to do it for us. This happens when we rightly believe who we are in Him. We walk in Grace and others see and glorify the Father. Led by His Spirit in how we talk, what we say, what our actions are, where we go, all of it in Him.

FOUR

Preach Grace, not war

MORE AND MORE WE are seeing ministries showing up on the Christian stage that highlight one or another of the signs, wonders, and miracles that are biblically supposed to follow any born-again believer. We in particular are seeing an influx of deliverance ministries. The leaders are certain these men and women of God whose declared "calling" is to cast out demons. Their focus is casting out demons. Suddenly, **they** are the anointed ones who have the revelation on how it is supposed to be done. Books are being written, podcasts are being made, and interviews and reels popping up. While it varies from one to another, they all have the metaphoric formula for how you cast out demons. Some even know hundreds of demons' names allegedly! So their, messages of spiritual warfare are validated by the exorcisms they do in the highly promoted and televised, social media meetings. I have met with pastors and leaders of some deliverance ministries over the years, even this past year. My question to them is always the same. Without accusation or criticism, I ask, “Why give demons a platform to perform on?”

No one has ever given me a direct answer. One person I talked to was sharing how they perform a deliverance session. The person described how the session was usually two or three hours long. I asked why it took them so long to expel evil spirits. The person I think thought they were talking to someone with little to no experience in deliverance ministry. And they were right partly. I don't have a deliverance ministry. I am in the ministry of preaching the Gospel of Jesus. When I told this person that I had cast demons out of people numerous times while ministering, and the demons flee and are cast out in anywhere from a few seconds to a couple minutes, they looked at me then in almost disbelief. I asked them again why it took them so long, and the person replied, it was just the way they had been taught. That's it right there!

The way they had been taught! Many are making a name for themselves making a ministry out of a gift. When we create doctrine or what I like to call “minister-ize” a particular gift that Jesus gives, we then begin to formulate how it works. Our focus then becomes about the gift rather than the One who gives the gift. Now don't hear what I am not saying. I believe people can be set free at some of these meetings and some are. But I think we miss out on glorifying Jesus, while we're busy giving the stage to demons to perform on. When we focus on the gift rather than the One who gives the gift, we see man made programs and formulas on how to. For instance, I interviewed three people who had went through a deliverance session of a known deliverance ministry. All three of them described how individually they went to a meeting at a set time. When they arrived, there was a mattress on the alter of the church. They were instructed to lay down on the mattress. Then a chair was placed at both ends of the mattress for the two people who who perform the deliverance. As they laid there each individually described how the two deliverance ministers read from a script. One said she was even struck on her back as one of the supposed ministers demanded that the spirit of Bobby (her ex-husband) come out of her. Another stated that they cast a demon out of her leg. One person told me that when she didn't manifest a demon, they began to call demons by name off a list they had to see if any demon would answer the roll call. This kind of nonsense is not of God, nor does it have any scriptural backing! In fact, summoning demons aligns them with witchcraft. All this because someone decided to make a formula on how to get freedom in Christ. Those three people told me that after their sessions, they felt exhausted, sore and did not believe anything good had come from it and no longer trusted that ministry. The exact opposite of what preaching the gospel is supposed to do happened because man got in the way and twisted what should be, into something they think is Godly. I knew the three people that went through this before hand. They didn't need deliverance from demons they needed healing from Jesus. They needed discipling on who they are in Christ. They are all free today in Jesus! Amen!

I would rather preach Grace than make war. Here's why from a scriptural standpoint under the new covenant of Grace.

We can rest in Him, with all authority as a son or daughter. When the enemy tries to bring an attack against us, we rest in the Lord, standing in His gifts that make up our identity in Him (the armor) knowing that the battle has already been won and we are so much more than conquerors in Christ. All we do, like Jesus, is speak the Word (the Truth/Sword of the Spirit) and it goes forth and tears down every lie of the enemy and "everything that exalts itself above the knowledge of God."

The Bible declares that as He (Jesus) is, so are we on the earth. That because of His Grace and gift of Righteousness, we reign with Christ in the earth. We can trust Grace, as our covenant to live fully under and submit to Him, free from the powers of sin and darkness. Knowing the only thing the enemy has now are lies, confusion, and accusations using the old law! The Bible says that "having disarmed the rulers and principalities, He made a spectacle of them" (Colossians 2:15). So when Jesus died on the cross having declared "it is finished", He disarmed the enemy of his power. The old law was replaced and the new covenant of His blood started. Since the power of sin is the law, in Christ (because He is Grace and through Him the covenant), we are no longer slaves to sin. Therefore, we no longer have to remain under the law. Grace came! Jesus did it all for us. It's all in Him! Even wisdom and knowledge. (Col 2:3)

When we preach the fullness of Grace, faith comes. When God's people begin to understand all that Jesus accomplished by the finished work of the cross, they begin to see who they are in Christ! They begin to know and believe that they have all authority over the enemy. Suddenly, where the enemy once influenced by using lies and condemnation, the believer now has authority in Jesus to pull down the stronghold and everything else that exalts itself against the knowledge of God.

When we preach the good news of the covenant of Grace, the believer begins to realize the same power that raised Christ from the dead, lives and dwells in them. And as they hear the words of Jesus and His word concerning who they are in Him, righteousness, co-heirs with Christ, sons and daughter of the Most High, whom He has justified and glorified! Then faith begins to come and that's when signs, wonders, and miracles begin to show up. That is also the moment in the life of an unbeliever when faith is received and the Holy Spirit convicts their heart of not believing, they can then believe, repent, and be born again. The greatest miracle of all! That's when the enemy is easily expelled from the place of influence, from the place of "demonizing" believers' and unbelievers' lives!

The moment faith comes, the supernatural can happen! Jesus never held hours-long deliverance sessions and neither do we need to when we are confident of who lives in us! I shared with another person that when demons begin to manifest in our meetings, I can't help but smile, maybe even laugh a little! I love kicking demons out of people's lives! But I will not allow them to distract from God being glorified! I will not tolerate them trying to distract from what the Holy Spirit is doing.

Have you ever noticed that it’s always amid the Holy Spirit doing something in people’s lives, that some demon wants to try and show out? People say “Pastor that’s just because the Holy Spirit is confronting them.” That can be true, but I would say that most of the time the little imp is just trying to distract from what the Lord is doing. They may not have realized it when they drudged themselves through the door, but the King of Glory lives in me. I am His dwelling place in which He dwells in by His Holy Spirit. The moment they show themselves they will immediately be dealt with, with the very authority of Jesus. You see that's whose authority we have. That's why we don't have to make war. Jesus already won!

The believer simply stands against the lies of the enemy through knowing who they are in Christ which includes understanding that the gifts of the armor He has given us are part of the makeup of our identity in Christ. That He lives in us by His Spirit is the other part. Jesus didn't fight Satan in the wilderness, He simply spoke the Word! He put satan in his place and there was nothing the devil could do except try again and then depart because he had to submit to the Lordship of Jesus. Jesus had been baptized in water, and then immediately by the Holy Spirit, and received power as the Father announced that Jesus was His Son in whom He was well pleased. Even before the cross, walking with the power of the Holy Spirit, the Word was all it took. While Jesus, a man under law at that point, was all alone in the wilderness with the devil it only took the Word empowered by the Holy Spirit in Jesus to route the enemy. Jesus demonstrated to us at that moment that the enemy had no power over Him.

Today He lives in us through His Spirit and the old covenant of law has been replaced by His new covenant of Grace! Himself, in us! So the same power that raised Jesus from the dead lives and dwells in us! Therefore we have power over the lies of the enemy. We have the authority to tell them to be quiet and stop distracting. In our meetings, I am very careful to ask Jesus about the timing of dealing with a manifestation of an evil spirit, because I don't want to do anything to take away from what the Spirit of God is doing in that moment.

There have been times when I have just told the demons to be quiet, and there have been times when the Spirit had me evict the demons almost as soon as they revealed themselves. When we follow the Holy Spirit in the meeting, then the Lord is glorified and people see the power of God at work either way. It's not a drawn out laborious battle between our will and the demons will. Someone once asked me why I was laughing when I was evicting some demons from a lady. I told them it was because it was a joyous moment, and I think it's funny that evil spirits get kicked out of people. It's joyous because that person is about to truly give their life to Jesus and be born again, or the believer is about to be free from the oppression and it's just fun to be used by Jesus in this way.

I do want to clarify something here I know the enemy has brought confusion to many believers about.. I want to start by asking this: If you were employed at a company and you knew your leadership from supervisor to the owner or CEO, and suddenly someone comes up to you wearing a uniform from your biggest competitor and they declare that you have to do what they tell you because they are your boss, are you going to just go along with them and do whatever they say? Are you even going to believe them? Of course not! Even if they are really convincing, and declare they bought the company!

You're not buying what they are selling. If they throw enough official-sounding rhetoric in there to make you start to wonder, what are you going to do? You're going to the one you know is in charge of you! So that you know the truth. So many believers have heard the doctrine that Christians can be demon-possessed. When we go to the Word of God, who is the boss at the top, we can clearly see that the Holy Spirit will not share a temple with an unclean or evil spirit. Not too long ago, I had a conversation with a pastor who had just counseled a believer with the Word, because they were under condemnation, and the enemy had almost convinced the person they had been possessed by a demon. This doctrine of man that is out there declaring that a Christian can be possessed by a demon, is a lie. Yes, I said that. It's a lie. The sad part is, like many others, the person teaching the doctrine, is most likely teaching something they were taught by someone else.

The Truth is that our God is a consuming Fire. Just as in the days of the law, the fire of God would consume what the high priest set in the holy of holies within the temple, when a person is truly born again, they are born of the Spirit. They are born into Christ. When they receive the Holy Spirit, the Spirit of God comes into that person and dwells within them. If there was an evil or unclean spirit in them, it is no longer there. Light and darkness do not mix. And Light always wins! Amen!

There is more teaching out there because so many self-proclaiming believers of Jesus are coming to the deliverance meetings and getting delivered, that Christians can be possessed. But it's simply not Truth. Even satan believes Jesus is Lord. Many people faithfully attend church and many have grown up in the same church that their grandparents or great-grandparents helped build even.

Many people attend a religious organization and proclaim they are Christians who have never been truly born of the Spirit. If you don't believe me, try attending a couple of your local churches. You know which ones, and just go sit anywhere you want. Wear a tank top and shorts and show your tattoo. Maybe you don't have a tattoo, in that case, wear a very nice suit, and pull up in an expensive car. Either way, you will see some people declare they are

Christians, but who they are is revealed upon your arrival. A decent person practicing a religion.

Many years ago, I was standing outside a church with a group of teenagers who were not the "churchgoing" kind. In fact, all of them were from homes where there was abuse, drugs, alcohol, and all kinds of evil at work. I know this because my wife and I with a couple of leaders would drive a bus to their side of town and pick them all up. But I was standing outside while several were smoking cigarettes. I watched as one of the church leaders walked across the parking lot and began to shame them for smoking on "the Lord's property". Telling them that they should respect the "house of God."

One brave young man, a young man whom my wife and I had personally been discipling for a couple of years at that point, stepped out from among the group before I could and said to the "leader", "Hey sir can I tell you something?" Holding up his cigarette to the man, he said "If this is the only thing I am still overcoming in my life right now, I am doing pretty good. You have no idea of what we have overcome with Jesus and what some of these other kids are still trying to get free from." The leader turned and walked away. I was so proud of that young man in that moment. The enemy was at work in that "Christian leader" to come bring condemnation and guilt with a good dose of shame to those teenagers. Many were just starting to receive the love of Jesus in their lives. Many had just started coming because they saw the change in their friends and how Jesus had transformed their lives.

It's not a hard argument it's a simple Truth. the Bible says, "They will know you are my disciples by your love for one another." It also says that that if a man says He loves

God but hates his brother, that man does not know God and the Truth is not in him. So yes, we have a lot of self-proclaimed Christians who like the Pharisees, are of their father the devil. They mask around as children of God but deny the power of God. But that doesn't mean Jesus doesn't love them and wants them to be delivered. Then there also some that just don't understand the Truth. They can't because they are under law. They have just been doing what they were taught. They believe Jesus is the Son of God and they believe God's Word is the Truth. They try hard to live by it and they struggle constantly with sin. All because they were taught the law and maybe a doctrine of grace. So they are still in bondage , going to the "house of God" faithfully every Sunday. All the while struggling in secret with trying to achieve a place of spiritualism in Christ that the pastors over them seem to have. They genuinely are trying hard, making the effort everyday, to be like Jesus. They too are faithful followers of the religion of Christianity. Yet they also because of the sin that over powers them fall into darkness and hidden sins. They inadvertently open doors to unclean or evil spirits in their lives and find themselves being demonized by them. If they continue to follow that path some end up possessed by the demon or demons they allowed in. These self-proclaimed religious people, or maybe it's better said, these people who follower and practice the religion of Christianity, could then be demon possessed. Why? The Bible declares there is a difference between lip service and true surrender. If we dug deeper into their lives it wouldn't take long to see they follow a religion rather than an actual relationship with Jesus. We would know by the fruit of their lives. That's why we see "Christians" possessed by demons.

Through the circumstance of the Spirit's orchestration, people who declare they are Christians as their religion, can find themselves possessed because of choices they give themselves to, or even because of circumstances they never intended to be caught up in. We see people who practice the religion of Christianity getting delivered from demonic possession because they are not born of the Spirit of God. They are just practicing a religion of their efforts.

There is also the other Truth that true believers, born-again believers filled with the Spirit of God, can be oppressed by an evil or unclean spirit. This is not possession. This is an evil or unclean spirit trespassing in a believer's life because that person has given up their authority in the area where the evil spirit is oppressing them. This could look like for example: a believer finds themself in a situation where they give into temptation to have sex with their boyfriend or girlfriend. Now because they opened that door, they find themselves dealing with guilt and shame, condemnation, and on top of that they have allowed that evil spirit to trespass in their life and constantly bombard them with the temptation to continue the sin by appealing to their lust of the flesh. It's a messy business, the things of the spirit realm, when we don't know what we are doing, or we choose to ignore the Spirit of God leading us. Now, not only is the enemy bringing condemnation, guilt, and shame for what you did, but he bates you to do it again by subtle accusations and further tempting thoughts. "You already crossed that bridge, might as well keep going!" Just so he can push you under law and condemnation. Why is this the tactic? Because the enemy knows that the power of sin is the law! So if he can keep you under the law, he can have that power of sin at work in your life. In all this, Jesus is our deliverer and when we turn to Jesus, He sets us free! We just need Jesus!

The Bible says that the weapons of our warfare are not carnal, but they are mighty for the pulling down of strongholds, and everything that exalts itself above the knowledge of God. The important word in this scripture is the word "warfare". It is the Greek word [strateia] which has its context in thought or strategic thinking. It does not have to do with somehow summoning spiritual strength to do battle in the spirit realm against principalities and rulers of the dark world. Remember, the Bible tells us that Jesus disarmed them and made a spectacle of them. But pastor, the Bible also says that "we wrestle not against flesh and blood...". Yes, Paul tells the believers this at the church of Ephesus, and the keyword here is the word *wrestle*. The Greek word is *palē*. But there is a verb and noun meaning here. Obviously, we don't literally wrestle demonic spirits. The Greek word can also mean struggle or contend with. So when we look at the context of the Word here and also in 2 Cor, we can see that what the Word is telling us is the enemy comes with lies and deception to try and rob us of our position.

Our identity in Christ with all the armor He brings to our lives allows us to stand against those rulers and principalities, as they sling the fiery darts of lies, confusions, condemnation and deception, even sickness or disease. We contend (palē) with them because we must contend with the flesh. They know we must contend with this flesh we live in, but so does Jesus! That's why the Word says "...and the life we now live in the flesh, we live through the Son of God." We live through faith in Jesus and the finished work of the cross. We withstand the enemy by believing we are who Jesus says we are in Him. Then we route the enemy by declaring the Word of God with authority and power.

Make no mistake my friend, it is not a war. It is strategically listening to the Holy Spirit who gives us discernment of evil spirits and reminds us of who we are and what the Word says. (Jesus is the Word). So we use God's power thinking strategically to pull down strongholds and anything that exalts itself against the knowledge of God. Anything that goes against what the Word says. It's fun! When the enemy thinks he has a plan and the Holy Spirit reveals it, we discern it, and then as a son or daughter of God, we command that it goes, stops, flees, releases a person, exits a person in the case of possession. Whatever the case, we have all authority under heaven and earth the Bible says. Whatever we bind on earth is bound in the spiritual realm and whatever we loose on earth is loosed.

Does this sound like warfare as we know it in our language? No, it sounds like to me we are in charge because of who is in us, and because of who we are in Him! The Bible says in Romans 5:17 "For if, because of one man's trespass, death reigned through that one man, much more **will those who receive the abundance of grace and the free gift of righteousness reign in life through the one man Jesus Christ.**"

We must preach Grace not war because we already reign over the enemy. When we are led to believe anything less, we are put back under law (accepting that the enemy has some kind of authority we must battle for) and we default to accepting less than what Jesus suffered and died for to give us this seat in heavenly places with Him. The enemy then can use that to bring more deception and lies, confusion, and condemnation into the life of a believer. Then they can't understand and they live a life of defeat always wondering why we do what we do and why sin continues to wreak havoc in their life. I am sick and tired of seeing believers living with guilt, shame, and condemnation. Fear having rule and they cannot see why. Why they don't walk in power? Why they don't step into all that God has purposed for them? When they pray and pray it just never seems good enough for God or at least nothing seems to change. When you know and believe the Truth, the Truth sets you free! The Truth is Jesus, and Jesus is Grace.

We have to preach the good news of Grace so that others will be set free, healed, delivered, and live victorious as sons and daughters reigning with Christ on the earth! Notice it says "Those ***who receive the abundance of Grace and His gift of righteousness*** reign in life through Jesus Christ." Until we know the Truth and believe who we are in Him, we won't take our proper place with Him. “Seated in heavenly places” at the “prepared table for me...” (us). The enemy has been defeated and we are no longer slaves to sin. The enemy just doesn't want them to know or believe this. The devil comes strategically as an angel of light and has infiltrated many of the church bodies around the world. Because he brought the old covenant of Law and mixed it into man's doctrine and wove law and grace together knowing that it nullified them both. When they are mixed they only bring forth religion that gives lip service but denies the power of God. That is why we have so many churches divided and so many believers living defeated lives under condemnation, guilt and shame, bound still by the power of sin.

FIVE

The faith that comes

WHY IS it so important pastor that we get this law and Grace issue resolved?

I'm glad you asked!

I'm sure you would agree that the Kingdom of God is lived now, right now, by faith in Jesus. But we need to understand how this faith comes to us, how faith arises or comes to anyone for that matter. I have had people ask me what some of the greatest miracles we have seen over the years, and for me some of the best is watching someone's countenance change as faith comes. While telling them the good news of His new covenant of Grace, while sharing that Jesus is Grace, while teaching what Jesus has done for us at the cross and on and on, suddenly you see **faith** coming to them. You see faith arising in them! When a person receives the gospel, God gives them a measure of faith! It comes because they believed the Truth. The moment you first believed the gospel, you received faith from God. When you put that faith in Jesus you are born again. Anytime someone hears the Truth preached and believes it, faith comes. When you have faith in Jesus, miracles can happen! Healing happens, freedom happens, restoration happens.

Paul, who the Lord used to write the gospel of Grace to the body of Christ in the Bible, saw something like this in Lystra. The Bible says in Acts 14 that Paul was preaching the good news and that while he was preaching he saw a man that had been crippled and couldn't walk since he was born. The Bible says that Paul looked intently at him and observed that he had **faith to be healed.** Paul said to him, "Stand upright on your feet!" The man jumped up and was instantly healed! What happened? Faith had come to this man. He heard the good news of Jesus and His new covenant of Grace being preached and faith came. Because of the words of **Christou** being preached, faith came! When he received the faith, the Holy Spirit gave Paul the discernment that it was there, so Paul told the man to get up. Paul wasn't there preaching on healing and how to be healed. He was simply preaching the gospel. Good news! There is now Grace we can live in. In Christ, we live in a new covenant established by His blood.

One of the first times I saw faith come, we were in Fairbanks, AK. A team of us was sitting in a coffee and bagel shop eating breakfast and reading the Word, praying about the next place the Lord was directing us to go. In walks this man who seemed to be content with life, happy even. He greeted us and we greeted him. That led to a 20-minute conversation with the gentleman. As soon as he saw our Bibles, he informed us that he was raised Lutheran but was now an atheist. It wasn't difficult to see that he had been hurt by his church, and had lost faith in what he had been taught and raised in. He boldly proclaimed his belief in "Mother Earth" and the beauty of the land. The Holy

Spirit spoke through several of us in response to various comments and as we went back and forth. The funny thing is, I only remember a few things from this conversation. I remember seeing faith beginning to arise in this man. After about 15 minutes he made this statement: "I will give you guys this, you're not like any Christians I have ever met." We said thank you and continued to talk a little more. We knew the Lord was talking right to this guy, on his turf, in a way that was making sense to him. The second thing I remember from this meeting was a supernatural moment at the checkout counter. The man finally said he had to go and thanked us for talking with him. As he turned to go pay for his food, the Lord spoke to me to get up and go pay for his meal. I knew we were there on this ministry trip on the Lord's financial provision, so whatever funds we had didn't matter. What mattered was that my King told me to get up and pay for the man's food and I love it when He asks or tells me to bless someone. So I promptly got up and walked over to the counter and told the cashier that I wanted to pay for his meal. The man promptly said no, and then said no again and again. But I handed my bank card to the lady and said yes absolutely. She took my card instead of his and began to swipe my card and process the payment. I could tell that the gentleman was staring at me, so I finally looked over at him and we locked eyes.

And at that moment I felt the literal presence of the Lord move past my shoulder into this man. I could almost see it with my natural eyes. This man, with our eyes locked and with a serious posture and almost a look of genuine disbelief said, "Why would you do that?" I immediately smiled and said because Jesus asked me to. The man shook my hand with a look of humbled questioning, picked up his bag of food, and said thank you. He then turned and walked out.

I knew at that moment the Lord had done something in that man's heart. The Spirit of the Lord moved past that man's defenses, his spiritual wall, because of an act of love. A kindness! Then as I turned to go sit back down and tell the team what had just happened, I saw Amy turn and look at me with a surprised look on her face. She then looked at my wife Cyndi and the others and said, "The Holy Spirit just told me that man's life was saved today!" As I sat down a peace just rested on us and I shared what happened at the register and how the Spirit of God just orchestrated the whole moment to touch this man's heart and restore faith in him.

Another time, we were in Denali, AK, and had walked into a shop. There was a lady behind the counter. Amy Kemp -who was part of the ministry team- was there and began to talk to her about the shop. The lady shared about her husband and her having just recently moved to California which spurred on more conversation about connections in California that Amy had. While they were talking, suddenly the Holy Spirit spoke to Amy. She asked the lady if she had any pain in her body. Right then I saw faith beginning to stir in the woman. She said, "Yes! All through my body every day. We have been to so many doctors and no one can tell me why I have this pain." Amy said to her, "Well, Jesus wants to heal you!" And that is where I saw faith come up in her. She was a believer, and people had prayed, she had prayed, and her husband had prayed. But with Jesus' words through Amy, the woman knew that there was no way these random strangers in her shop could have known that about her. It was Jesus speaking through this woman. And when she heard the word from Jesus that He wanted to heal her, faith came! Amy said, "Can we pray for you?" And the woman immediately said yes. We laid hands on her and prayed. Guess what happened? Thats right! She was instantly healed. All the pain left her body immediately and she began to cry and rejoice.

You see my friend, the Bible says that Jesus is the author and perfecter of our faith. Romans 10:17 says that "faith is from hearing and hearing through the words of Christ." Notice that I did not quote the KJV translation of "...and hearing of the Word of God". That's because when we look at the original Greek manuscript here, it uses two words that are vitally important for our understanding of how faith comes. The Greek uses the word "Rhema" which means *the spoken or declared word*, and it also says "by the words of Christou" which is Christ. This brings a clear understanding that faith comes from the Good News. The Gospel of Jesus, which is the new covenant of Grace!

Ever noticed anyone get excited when they hear someone telling them how God struck down someone with a disease, or how about when the bear attacked the kids for making fun of the prophet? What about when God added more and more laws to the old covenant of law and there was more and more people had to do to please God? I bet we would be excited if we had to raise goats and sheep or go purchase the best we could afford to take to the priest once a year to atone for our sins! What about when the preacher says, "The wrath of God is stored up for the sinner, and if you're not right with God, if you have sin in your life when you die you will face that wrath!" No, of course not! Why? Because the law brought and still brings condemnation and death.

But Jesus brought a new way, a new hope! Jesus took all our sins and infirmities on himself and was punished for us on the cross! For all our sins, forever, were judged and punished in the body of Jesus! He did that so that we could be redeemed back to the Father without fear of punishment, or shaming! So that in hearing He says in His word, there is now no condemnation in Him for those that believe, we would receive His gift of righteousness and Grace. So that we could be grafted into the Family of God guilt-free. He delighted in doing this for us so that He could give us His gift of Righteousness and institute Himself as Grace! A "new covenant of His blood". That is the best news we could hear in our lifetime.

When we preach the good news, Hope begins to speak through us, and when people who do not yet believe hear words about Jesus and what He has done, about His blood that was shed and the finished work of the cross. When people hear that God is no longer mad at them or that God isn't punishing them for their sinful ways, they begin to have hope and faith begins to come alive in them. When faith, even just a tiny amount the size of a mustard seed is received big things can happen. The Holy Spirit can move past their pride, past their walls of defense from hurt and insecurities, and convict their heart of unbelief. Suddenly, they believe and they surrender their life to Jesus. They take that faith that has come and they put it in Jesus. At that moment, when they now believe in their heart and confess with their mouth that Jesus is Lord, they are born again. Faith came and as a result, they chose to believe Jesus! So in the spiritual realm, they are born again, now born into Christ. No longer of Adam.

It's a beautiful picture of how when we preach the good

news, people who receive that good news, then receive faith from the Lord and believe. They put their faith in Jesus. Hearing through the words of Jesus they receive faith. It still stirs me up today. This is why Paul exclaimed "I am not ashamed of the gospel, for it is the power of God unto salvation!" [In the Greek the word soterō meaning deliverance from all sin, evil, infirmity and anything not of God.]

Another time my wife Cyndi and I sat next to a man on a flight and as we sat down he was pleasant and greeted us. Within a few minutes, he was telling us that he was a Jew. He explained to us the various levels of their faith in Judaism and how he was more a bottom-ringer kind of Jew, but that he had grown up practicing the covenant of law following their beliefs. To keep a long story short, about an hour into our conversation, I'm sharing the Gospel of Grace, the new covenant with him. We realized that he had stopped talking, had turned in his seat to face us more, and was intently listening. We also realized that the presence of God was resting on us all as we spoke to him. He just finally kind of shook his head and I will never forget what he said to us. He shared that there were not a lot of Jewish girls where he was from, and so he had dated a lot of Christian ladies and attended their churches over the years. He said, "I never understood what the preachers would mean by their sermons. I knew the law, and they were adding all this other stuff to it and it just never made sense to me." Then he said, "But what you guys are telling me makes perfect sense! You have to keep doing what y'all are doing because I can believe what you're saying!"

What happened? Faith came!

By the time we landed, this Jewish man who had been

raised always trying to keep the law, but desperately failing, told us that he was going to start reading in the Bible in Romans and that he could not believe he had never heard of the new covenant of Grace. His whole countenance was different! My wife and I were blown away! This man believed and confessed that he could believe this! We did not try and lead him in some "sinner's prayer", we simply shared the good news with him and he believed. Faith came alive in him because he received the gospel we were sharing with him and he will decide whether to put that faith in Jesus or not. The Holy Spirit did not prompt us to do anything else. Isn't that beautiful? We were not trying to **get him saved.** That is not our job! Our job is to preach the gospel so that in hearing they can believe and receive their portion of faith. Then as the Holy Spirit convicts them of not believing they will choose to put their faith in Jesus and receive Him, and His covenant of Grace. To add just a bit more emphasis, I want to share one more story of watching the miracle of the faith that comes.

This one is a little bit closer to home for me. When the Lord began revealing Himself as Grace to my wife and me, it was like we had been preaching the meal, without fully understanding how the meal had been prepared. We just knew that the Lord was good. We knew that He had asked us years ago to just love them, concerning His church. We had learned a lot choosing to follow the Holy Spirit early on in ministry, over doctrine or men's opinion. But like someone who goes to a person's house for a five-star meal, we just accepted that Jesus was the way and we enjoyed some of the meal. Not having a lot of understanding of how intricate the ingredients were and how delicately the Chef had woven them together and took precious care to remove anything that would ruin any part of the meal. So we raised our children in the knowledge of the Lord and raised them to know the authentic presence of God, the Holy Spirit. Our children know the peace of God and they honor the Lord above anything else. We have been so blessed in that area. But as the Lord took us on that show and tell, and began to reveal the fullness of the finished work of the cross, revealing the gospel of Himself as Grace.

We watched our faith begin to grow more and more. To a place that we can't help but tell anyone willing to listen and receive. That leads me to a night out on the town with our kids one evening when we ran into a young lady who had attended off and on our Friday night *Life180* meetings. We hadn't seen her at a meeting in several months. She knew about our previous ministry trip from social media and asked how our trip had gone. We began to share with her about the various miracles and healings that Jesus had done through all of us on the team on the trip. Then we began to share the revelations the Lord had given us in the months prior and all that He had spoken to us and shown us about the Gospel of Grace. My daughter Kynzie was standing here with us as we were talking. Once again, miracles were happening.

As this young lady listened and began to receive the good news, we watched as her literal countenance began to change. Much like when you give anyone good news about something they thought was hopeless, her expression began to change. Faith was beginning to arise inside of her! You might say, “Pastor, if she was a believer, didn't she already have faith?” The answer to that is of course yes! However, the Bible says in 2 Corinthians 3:18 that with the veil being removed by Jesus, we are going from glory to glory. When we turn to Jesus and receive His covenant of Grace, the veil is removed and we are set free from the law of sin and death. No longer slaves.

But as we grow more and more in our understanding of the fullness of Grace, led by the Spirit of God into all Truth, we grow. What grows with that? Faith! Jesus authors our faith and sees us through to the finish line where we will one day step into eternity and be with Him. He perfects our faith as we walk with Him, and follow His lead, His Holy Spirit. So yes, believers' faith can grow and should be growing.

I am hoping that as you are reading this book, your faith is growing, as well as you turn your eyes to Jesus and are stirred in your spirit man that Jesus has done so much more than you have been taught.

After we said our goodbyes to this young lady, my daughter and I got into my car to head home. As I was driving down the road, my daughter looked at me and said, "Hey Dad, I get it now." I said, “What do you mean?” She said, "What you said to that lady, everything you said, I get it now. It all makes sense!" I just smiled and said that's awesome baby girl! I was trying to watch the road but felt the warmth of tears building in the bottom of my eyelids. It didn't take long until the warm flow of tears coming down my face turning to cold moisture on my cheeks could be felt. I quickly wiped my eyes and said to my daughter again, "That's awesome." She said, "I mean you and mom taught us most all that, but I have just never heard you say it in a way that made perfect sense to me about Jesus and Grace, I think y'all need to keep preaching that."

It was amazing to see that faith was stirred and grew in my daughter just by listening as I was sharing the gospel with another person. I will never forget that night. When I got home and shared that with my wife and what our daughter had said, we both shared a moment of tearful thanksgiving. The Lord again stirred our faith that as our daughter was getting ready to go off to college, He had her and was teaching her all things. Parents never give up, and never say you messed things up too much to share the good news with your kids! No matter how old they are! There is power in the gospel! The Bible says, "Power unto Salvation!" The power of God in the good news brings faith. The faith that comes when they hear it and receive it will be the faith that will release the supernatural transforming power of God to set free, heal, deliver, and restore them. It is also the same faith for those who believe that will grow more and more as they become fully under Grace and no longer under the condemnation of the old law and its ways. Freedom in Christ is the result! More and more, from glory to glory.

SIX

Can't have what you can't see

I DON'T KNOW if you noticed, but in several of the previous testimonies, there was a common statement made by the various people. "That makes sense!" Now I know, before we get too far into this, someone is already looking at the chapter title and saying to themself, "But I thought faith included "the evidence of thing not yet seen". So pastor why are you saying we can't have it if we can't see it?"

I'm so glad you asked! I am not referring to Hebrews 11:1 in this chapter title. I'm referring to 2 Corinthians 3, where the Bible tells us even today when the law is preached, it puts a veil over the people's hearts and they can not understand the truth. They can not see with the eyes of their heart because there is a veil over their heart. So because they can not understand the truth when the law is preached, they can't receive the Truth. When the law is preached, it prevents someone from understanding what Jesus has done for them, they don't fully understand the Word of God, and they often don't understand really what the pastor preached on. Even if the preacher is preaching about something in the New Testament, but adds in a little law as the how to get it, or the must do to have it, that little bit of "leaven ruins the whole batch". Remember the Jewish man on the plane? He said it didn't make sense to him because the preachers were preaching law mixed with a new way and he couldn't understand it. I took a survey years ago at a church where I was on staff. I went around to as many of the church members as I could after the service was over and asked them one simple question: "What did the pastor preach about?"

It would blow your mind the answers that people gave me. I remember the percentage of people who could tell me the main point of the sermon immediately following the service was less than 10%. Some would give me a quick catch line or a word or two that they thought summed up the entirety of the message. Of course, there were a few who happily whipped out their notes! But who's counting that? LOL. It was interesting because these were people who would fight and defend the pastor if someone spoke ill of him. They were faithful attendees every Sunday. Some of them were part of the volunteer leadership team. What I did hear a lot of were statements like "I don't remember everything, but the illustration was cool and made his point well." I would hear people say things like, "I will probably have to listen to the recording again this coming week!" And even statements like "If I'm being completely honest, I didn't understand it all, but I know it was good!"

Back then the survey wasn't done from a perspective of law being preached. However, looking back now, with the knowledge and understanding that mixing the two covenants of the old law and Grace ruined both for the chance to work in someone's life. And the primary reason was their hearts were veiled. They didn't have a chance and so many even today still under law, just don't know. No wonder God said my people perish for a lack of knowledge. Although God said this to the priest through the prophet Hosea, because the priests themselves didn't know God, it still is a fact today! Many believers walk around in condemnation, guilt, and shame, powerless, because they do not know, or cannot understand the Truth! The sad part of this is we have "priests" today who do not know, or worse, do not believe in themselves and continue to preach law or law and Grace mixed! Yet the law cannot set anyone free, and although the law is holy, it was not given to make anyone holy. And when the gospel is preached, mixed with even a little bit of the law or its ways, it ruins the whole batch! This is the very thing that Paul is addressing with the church in Galatia!

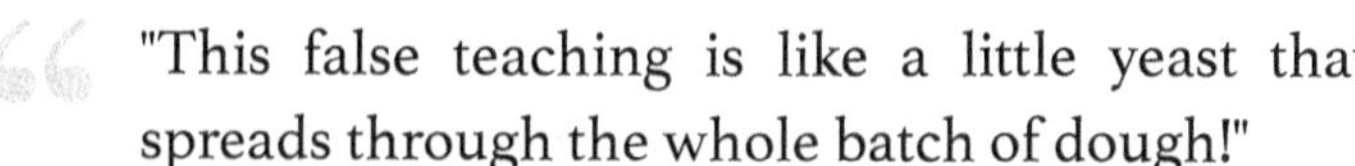

> "This false teaching is like a little yeast that spreads through the whole batch of dough!"
>
> Galatians 5:9 NLT

Paul was upset about what was happening in the church because they had received the Truth, the good news of the covenant of Grace, and put their faith in Jesus and the finished work of the cross, they had believed all that Paul had taught them. Then some Pharisees came along and told the people that they must continue to obey the covenant of law also. So now they were mixing law and Grace and people in the church were falling into sin and all this stuff was happening that they had been set free from! The minute the law of condemnation and death was mixed back in, it immediately empowered sin in the people's lives and left them powerless and feeling guilt and shame. So Paul is asking them who bewitched you? This mixing of the old with the new is bad! And it only takes a little law to ruin it all!

I imagine many of you can identify with this. I know I did not too long ago. The thing is, the enemy only has this option to try and use against us. If he can get us back under the law, or keep us under the law, then sin has power over us. We will try our best to live right and please God and we will always fail in this futile effort. And when we fail, the guilt comes and shame begins to move us from the place we have been given by Jesus. We start to think, man I worked hard all week and I need to just rest instead of going to meet with the other believers. Church or meetings are not the first to go though, before we stop we have usually already stopped spending that secret place time with the Lord. We know we messed up and the enemy accuses us and our conscience condemns us, so we pull away from the intimacy we used to have with Jesus. We stop talking to Him, and we shut out His voice. We prioritize other things over His presence. Then we stop going to church because the enemy has told us the lie "If they only knew what I did" and "God's already mad at me for what I did, if I go to church then I'm a hypocrite and God is going to be mad at me!" So when a preacher preaches a different gospel, when the law is mixed with Grace, it veils, and people cannot understand the Truth, and the power of sin comes from the law, so now sin is continually at work in the lives of so many believers, and so condemnation comes and it's the cycle of religion that in the ends ruins and even destroys people's lives.

This is why it is so important to rightly divide the word of God, the old law from the new covenant. Because when the gospel is preached and someone turns to Jesus and receives His gifts of salvation, His gift of righteousness, and is born again into Christ, to then preach to them the old law ways then is bewitching them! Can you imagine being told, you are forgiven! You are a new creation! That the Father sent His Son Jesus to take the punishment of your sins and the blood of Jesus has washed you white as snow! And then in the next sermon tell them they will be cursed if they don't tithe? If they don't obey God this is why God allows you to get sick and even puts sickness on some to teach them to obey! What about preaching that if they want to be blessed by God then they need to be a blessing to someone else? Can you see the confusion? Can you see how mixing law with Grace ruins it all? Family this must stop. Either we believe Jesus finished the work at the cross and sat down at the right hand of the Father and He has done for us all that we could never have done, or we all need to get a complete copy of the Torah and start working hard to memorize the law. Because the Bible says that if you violate one law you have violated them all. If this is the case why did Jesus come?

Thank you Jesus that You did come! And when we accept the new covenant of His blood and turn to Jesus, put our complete faith in Him, when we fully surrender to the King of kings, the veil is removed and He opens the eyes of our hearts. He removes the stony heart that the law is written on, and He gives us a heart of flesh, born again into Christ. We now see all that He has done, and how He loved us, so we love Him and receive His gift of righteousness. Grace becomes our home. He lives in us, our new Covenant, by His Holy Spirit. We were crucified with Christ, and we no longer live, but Christ lives in us! And this life we now live in the flesh we live through the Son of God.

SEVEN

The unforced rhythms of Grace

WE WERE SO tired and yet there was a strength in us all. We had slept in our rented SUV from about 1 am until 7 am at the border crossing because who knew international border crossings closed at 11 pm! We had arrived at 12:30 am and in the middle of nowhere. After getting back into the United States (a miracle all by itself), we drove to this little town named Haines in the southeastern area of Alaska. We could not believe that we slept in the rental car and woke up feeling refreshed. It was refreshing from the Lord because our physical bodies were still trying to figure out what just happened. But here we were in Haines, Alaska, this beautiful town set in mountainous terrain on an inlet ocean view. It was a picturesque scene better than any Hollywood movie could have shown. We found the local breakfast diner and ate what we thought was probably the best breakfast on the planet at that time.

After eating and talking about what Jesus was saying to us as a team to go do, it was unanimous, that we would walk the town and just see who Jesus put in our path on this day.

We paid our bill and stepped out onto the sidewalk. Beautiful mountains surrounded us on every side. We decided to take a group picture. As we were trying to position ourselves in the middle of the street for the perfect mountain-filled background, a couple came walking towards us. They asked if we would like them to take the picture for us. So of course, we agreed and thanked them! They took the pictures for us. Then we all introduced ourselves. As we were talking the Lord gave a word of knowledge to one of our team members. She promptly spoke up and asked the man if he had pain in his right ankle. Of course, we knew at that moment the Lord was up to something. The man seemed hesitant and a little stumped, and said no. His wife immediately looked at him crazy and said, "Yes he does! He has pain all the time from an injury 20 years ago!" We all gave a laugh and the man then admitted he did suffer from pain in his right ankle.

Then Courtney, the team member the Lord had given the word of knowledge to, told the man that Jesus wanted to heal his ankle and asked if we could pray for Him. He said yes. So we prayed and the man was immediately healed. His wife then started crying and asked if we could pray for her brother who was back home in Texas and fighting cancer. So we prayed again. We talked a little more and they explained they were there in Haines because they had just moved the wife's mother to Haines where she was retiring. They went on to explain she had a heart condition and high blood pressure and she had decided to leave Texas and move to this quiet and peaceful little town to live out the rest of her days. We went on to walk the town. As the Lord led we went from talking and praying with another man who was an alcoholic and had run from God and the law to this little remote town in Alaska, to one shopkeeper to another. Praying and revealing the glory of God to the people the Holy Spirit led us to. It was so easy! We were going from place to place in His rest and strength and Jesus was encountering people along the way, meeting them right where they were.

I walked into one shop, it was a quaint little clothing resale shop. The moment I walked in and saw the lady behind the counter, the Spirit of God inside me began revealing two things. One she was the owner and second, she was oppressed by the enemy and was having financial problems with her shop. I immediately went over to her and greeted her. I asked her how she was doing today and she replied she was good. To which I immediately said what I heard Jesus saying through His Holy Spirit. I told the woman that she wasn't good, and that she had been having a hard week, that Jesus wanted her to know, that He sees her and has heard her cry. The Lord went on to say that the weightiness of oppression she had been feeling was lifting that He was turning the financial issues around and that the Lord was about to bless her business! This woman had crocodile-sized tears coming down her face and began to tell me how she couldn't believe Jesus would send me there to tell her all this and how I could not have known any of it. How she had been praying and feeling like God didn't see her or hear her.

I smiled and said, "Well now you know!" I looked over and saw a red plastic set of sunglasses on her counter for sale. They were marked $2. I said I wanted to buy the sunglasses and took out two one-dollar bills. The lady said not to pay her but I insisted. By this time two of our team members had come into the shop as well. I turned around and walked towards one of the team members and as if on some kind of cue, a large group of people came through the door of the shop! They were talking and laughing and went straight to the clothing and began picking out dresses and clothes, looking at shoes, and picking out items to buy. I just laughed! Jesus was just showing out His glory! I looked back at the shop owner and smiled. She was just in awe. She shared more with us about her church and relationship and we prayed with her before leaving. We went on and continued to be used by the Lord. A lady was healed of scoliosis she had since birth and a stomach disease that had almost killed her the year before, another lady healed of pain in her leg, another lady declared while we were all praying for her heart problems, "Oh my gosh I just felt something leave my chest!".

In all, 8 people were healed of infirmities, and many more were touched by the Lord, all in 35 minutes of walking this little town. Then, we stopped at a point after talking and praying with a man, and we all felt it! We were done there! It was time to go. As we were talking later, Amy said, "There is a rhythm to when the Spirit of the Lord is moving. And when He is done, the rhythm lifts!" It was a perfect description. There was this unseen rhythm to walking by the Spirit of the Lord and being used to reveal His glory on the earth! It wasn't forced upon us, we just said yes! We didn't strive to go out and find people to tell them about Jesus, He just put people in our path as we went because we fixed our eyes on Jesus and went where He led us with purpose, knowing we were there to be used by Him, for Him and through Him. Life with Jesus, our covenant of Grace, being led by His Spirit is restful and unforced. We get to choose to be used for His glory. It's simply yes, Lord. And He does the rest. I love how the Message translations put it in Matthew 11:28-30:

> "Are you tired? Worn out? Burned out on religion? Come to me. Get away with me and you'll recover your life. I'll show you how to take a real rest. Walk with me and work with me—watch how I do it. Learn the unforced rhythms of grace. I won't lay anything heavy or ill-fitting on you. Keep company with me and you'll learn to live freely and lightly."

When we choose to fully surrender to Jesus, and know who we are in Him, we can live in His rest! We can abide in unforced rhythms of Grace as He leads us through our day, through seasons of life, and mountains and valleys by His Spirit. He will teach us and show us, He will use our lives to reveal His glory in the earth, and as we fix our eyes on Jesus each day we will go from glory to glory in an unforced rhythm of Grace.

EIGHT

Grace in wilderness

OUR WORD WILDERNESS is the word "midbar" in Hebrew which comes from the Hebrew word "dabar". Interestingly enough there are several other words associated with the same root word. "Dibra" means Spoke, "Diber" means commandment, and "Davar" means spoken word. It's interesting because where *midbar* is used in the Old Testament are all times when God brought His people into a desert place, and it was always to speak to them, teach them, and lead them to the next place. In Greek, the word for wilderness is the word "Eremos". Similar to the Old Testament, every time this word is used in the New Testament it is a place of solitude, not inhabitable, a temporary retreat to a place of silence, where Jesus spoke to the Father, and where others would go to listen to what God wanted to speak to them.

So many times we as believers, have found ourselves in a place where there was nothing for us. Where it was like we were in a dry desert with little or nothing to sustain us, not able to see God at work and feeling like we were alone. . We have often misconstrued those times as spiritual attacks, times where God was "testing us". We have heard it preached even that our sins have led us to the wilderness so we need to get right, and repent so God will forgive us and take us back to the promised land! I imagine there will be many reading this who will say "That's right pastor" and immediately remember hearing something like that taught from the pulpit. What if I told you that was all wrong?

I remember when I was just a child. It was in the middle of my second-grade school year that my mom suddenly packed up my two sisters and me and moved us to a different place. A place away from my dad. I remember it seemed a little weird to me, and I missed my dad, but the place wasn't scary to me. It didn't seem to me to be much different than where we had come from as far as the location. We lived in a house. We met some new people who lived in the house with us. They had kids too our age that we got to play with. My dad came to see us and even brought me a dirt bike on one of his first visits after we had first moved. A little while later we moved in with my uncle and his girlfriend. That was kind of fun. He was nice to us and even took me shooting when I was just six years old. Let me shoot his .357 magnum revolver. Man, that thing did have a kick! Later we moved to this cool gigantic house. I mean it was a little different than the other places. We had to go upstairs to get to our house. It had a playground in the outside area, that was surrounded by everyone else's houses. After a little while we moved to this cool little metal box-shaped house. It was in a little circle drive place with other long box-shaped metal houses. There were some cool people always hanging out with their loud motorcycles. Working on their motorcycles and revving them up. I had to stay in my little front yard to play with my

GI Joe action figures. But I also got to walk home from school to the building behind my house. It was really neat. My friend and I and my sister who walked home with me, would go into the building to say hello to my friend's mom who worked there. There were cool pool tables and this long counter with all these glasses and cool-looking bottles on a shelf. We would go to the back where my friend lived with his mom and hang out and play Atari video games for a little while and then go home. When we got home, usually my mom would have peanut butter sandwiches for us or bologna sandwiches. Sometimes we would get a bucket of fried chicken! But my favorite times were when we could go and get a happy meal from McDonald's.

You see as a child, I had no idea there was anything wrong. I had no idea that my mom had left my dad and filed for a divorce. I had no idea that those cool houses with friends and my uncle were just nice people taking in a woman and 3 children who were homeless. I never knew as a child that we were living in government or low-income housing. I didn't know I was hanging out in a bar after school or that the trailer home in the little trailer park was below the poverty line and we lived next door to motorcycle gang members who were most likely trafficking drugs and guns. All I knew was where I lived, my mom was there to take care of us and feed us, love us, and protect us. I would later understand why my mom carried a pistol in her purse at all times and I later understood that everyone else would consider the way we lived, where we lived, and how we lived, a wilderness time in our lives. But as a child, I never saw it that way. It wasn't until I was much older also that I learned how the Lord provided for us continually in that wilderness.

There are numerous places throughout the scriptures

where people are in the wilderness. For various reasons, but the common denominator in every scenario, is God is there with them. Leading them, speaking to them, and providing for them. In the Old Testament, in Exodus, He leads them through the desert and eventually into the promised land. While they are in the desert He takes care of them. Teaches them and speaks to His people through the leaders and priests. In the New Testament, we see Jesus go to the desert to pray, we see He was led there by the Spirit at one point where Satan even tried to hijack His time of fasting by coming and tempting Jesus. Which didn't work. But we also see how the Father took care of Jesus and tended to Him after His fast. Others were found in the wilderness at times hearing from the Lord. You see the children of Israel, even today see Midbar not just as a desert land, but as a place where God speaks. We also see in the scriptures several places where we are told to fix our eyes on Jesus. To fix our thoughts on things above. The Bible speaks of a child-like faith!

What's your point, pastor? My point is this: Grace is always in the wilderness with us. Jesus, who is Himself our new covenant of Grace, never leaves us or forsakes us, but moreover, that is because today because of the finished work of the cross, He is in us. When we are led into wilderness times in our lives, while following the Holy Spirit, we can know that the Lord wants to speak or reveal something to us. It's a meeting place. When we fix our eyes on Jesus, a wilderness season is just a season where we are led to a place where we don't have the distractions that life throws at us. The busyness of the day, the constant of friends and activities. The truth is, when it comes to following Jesus, with our eyes fixed on Him, our thoughts on things above,

Kingdom things then no matter where we are we continue to follow Him and Trust Him. Like a child who didn't know he was "poor" because Jesus provides, Jesus heals, Jesus speaks, Jesus listens, Jesus comforts, Jesus delivers, strengthens, leads, and guides us by His Spirit, we look continually to Him. If we have truly fixed our eyes on Jesus we can go through anything in life and Grace is there. Grace is in the wilderness.

Chances are, we may not even realize where we are, would be considered by others a "wilderness", because we are so satisfied by Jesus and what He provides, nothing else matters. It's childlike. This is why it's important to listen to what the Lord is speaking and follow His voice. See what His Word says about how to live in Grace. Grace will take you through life, all its ups and downs, and produce gratefulness for it all. When all we see is Grace in every circumstance, we won't see what others see in their natural eyes. We won't see lack, because in Jesus there is no lack! When our eyes are fixed on Jesus, we walk in gratitude for all He has done, and all that He does for us. It changes our perspective. We will walk through wildernesses and not think anything is wrong. We will walk on mountain tops and stay humble. We will walk into dark places and fear not. We will walk into places where people are sick and deliver His gift of healing. We walk as He is, because so are we in the earth.

I believe as we wrap up this chapter, that there are many out there in a wilderness place right now. I want to tell you this is your shift. Take your eyes off the circumstances. The circumstances are why you believe you're in a wilderness place. The enemy wants your eyes on the circumstances. I want to encourage you today, to put your eyes on Jesus.

Just say this with me: "Jesus, today I look to you. I fix my eyes on you. Not just an imaginative thought of you the person, my eyes on all that You are and have done for me. Today Jesus, I remember Your gift of righteousness you gave me, and that I am a son or daughter in our Father's Kingdom. Because of what You did for me, I have an inheritance of promises. So today I thank you for what I need and I receive it in faith from you. Father, I thank you in Jesus' name for meeting my every need, and because my faith is fully in Jesus I receive it as it is already done for me. Amen".

NINE

The anti-Grace mind

> "For the **mind** that is set on the flesh is hostile to God, for it does not submit to God's law; indeed, it cannot."
>
> Romans 8:7 ESV

IF YOU'RE like me then the first question here is, who in their right mind would be anti-Grace?

Well, the scriptures tell us that we all have the potential to be anti-God. When we have not yet received the fullness of the Truth, the gospel of Jesus, the new covenant of His blood, Grace. You see my friend we have a problem in today's church. While there are remnants of believers living through Jesus daily by His Spirit, there are so many believers who have not been taught that what Jesus did in going to the cross established a new covenant for us to live in Him through His Spirit in us.. They have not been taught about the finished work of the cross. They have heard of the term most likely, because it is used in talking about salvation, but the complete work goes way beyond just the fact He died on the cross for us. So many have not learned how to live fully under Grace, and to make matters worse, many churches, denominations, and evangelists continue to preach the old law and its ways as part of how to live for God and please God. How to be holy and be more spiritually mature.

There are many still preaching you will be cursed if you don't tithe. Many churches today don't preach the infilling of the Holy Spirit. There are varying teachings about how you get the Holy Spirit when you say the sinner's prayer and mean it. There are teachings that the Holy Spirit doesn't exist today on the earth! Not sure how they prove that with so many supernatural happenings in the body of Christ around the world and from a Biblical standpoint for that matter.

Then some churches preach we have to be "filled up". Think about that for a minute. It's the Holy Spirit that lives and dwells in us. The Spirit of the Lord. Jesus by His Spirit in us. What? Does He somehow weaken through the week? And you mean to tell me that your church is the place where the Holy Spirit chose to recharge Himself in us? Like His power barely gets some people from Sunday to the next Sunday? For others, they have to get a refill by Wednesday night or they won't make it to Sunday. "You better get to the House of God, if you don't you won't make it out there."

The problem with all of these things is this! They cause us to set our mind on ourselves to figure out what God wants, or what we need to grow more or become more like Him. They leave us focusing on achieving by what we do, to become holy, to get right with God. So we have people running to the alters because a pastor said, "You need to search your heart and you need to repent and get right!" So immediately as we search, our conscious condemns us! When we do these things it sets our mind on the flesh's ability to accomplish the scriptures they throw out, as mixing the old law and its ways with Grace will make us more Godly. Yet the Bible tells us that a mindset on the flesh is hostile to God! So we make an effort in ourselves and we run to the altar hoping that this is the one! This time it's going to work. Only to greet Monday morning with the same person in the flesh as we were the week before.

How many times have we seen a believer striving to become a better Christian? Whether that was through reading more of the Bible, volunteering for more service involvement at the church, or going to prayer meeting after prayer meeting! What about attending more spiritual enrichment classes at the church the pastor said if you want to do ministry in this church you have to complete these classes. How about the oldie, God helps those who help themselves. No matter how hard we try, we just end up doing what we want, we get mad because we prayed and prayed and nothing changed. We practically ran to that altar and begged God to forgive us one more time. We cried and snorted on the prayer partner down at the front. We attended all the classes and we gave every last dime to the church, the pastor never put you in a place of leadership and now you barely attend church and your prayer time is just a venting session to God about how nothing ever works out and you feel guilty because you still struggle with the same sin in your life that you were before you took all the classes, went to prayer and gave all your money to the church.

The problem is, on our best day, there is nothing we can do in our flesh to please God. Our mind when set on the flesh cannot submit to God. Cannot submit to the leading of the Holy Spirit, especially if we wrongly believe that He does not exist on the earth today, or that He doesn't dwell within us. We cannot submit to the leading of the Spirit if our mind is on the circumstances surrounding us, we cannot hear His voice when all we hear is our conscience condemning us as the old law is written on our hearts and the law that is preached to us every service or online through various social media brings a veil to our hearts. Our flesh can't meet the righteous requirements of God by trying to obey Him all day long every day. No one has ever done it, except Jesus! You see?

A lot of times we think we have to fight the enemy harder because he just seems to be kicking your tail. But the problem is, as long as you are under the law, he doesn't have to do much except keep you there. Trust me friend he is happy to let a lot of you stay in your church. The devil knows the power of sin is the law. So if he can just keep you under the law by a little accusation here and there, a bowl full of condemnation when you do sin, along with a nice tall cold glass of guilt to top it off, then the law will do the work for him. So he is happy to come as an angel of light, and "convict you of your sins" every time you mess up. He knows you will have to run to church on Sunday to get right with God. He knows that if you believe you have to get to church, go to a prayer meeting, or need a worship song to play to "get filled up", then you will be under the law for the rest of your life. As long as you believe this is how it is done, you will have your mind on your flesh to please God. And it will never be good enough. So you will stay in the cycle. Never truly receiving the fullness of Grace and being set free. The idea that we don't have to do anything to please God is the point of Grace coming for us. Jesus did it all and people stay in this anti-Grace mind until they get this revelation.

The anti-Grace mind is not someone whose mind is just set on the flesh. It's also someone who has been taught law and Grace mixed. So their mind is on the flesh for "Godly, spiritual reasons!" They don't realize their heart is veiled and they can't understand the Truth. It's someone who believes they have to do something to please God. It's someone who is blinded by religious doctrine and probably thinks they are living a Godly life. They go to church every time the doors are open. They believe that if you want to be holy, you have to do your part to live holy. They believe if they pray enough then God will heal them maybe. The anti-Grace mind is a person who will get mad when you tell them that to preach tithing as a doctrinal truth to live by, no longer exists because it was of the law. It's a person who believes if you want to get closer to God you have to pray more, read your Bible more, or live a vagabond-style life of poverty. It's a person who preaches that playing instruments in church is a violation of God's word. It's a person who says, "It's ok to live how I want because I am under grace!" It's a person who says anything about you must do this if you want God to bless you or heal you. Well, pastor how can you say all this?! It's simple my friend, if there was anything we could do to earn God's love and goodness, if there was anything we could do in or of ourselves to please God and meet his requirements, then why did Jesus need to come? All these old law ways of teaching, shift our mind from the goodness of God, His blessings, favor, healing, provision, redemption, power, and presence to our abilities in our flesh to perform or achieve. If you have only known preaching of law and grace mixed, then you have heard about how it's supposed to be all this goodness but it's not an everyday occurrence in your life, let alone your complete way of life! You see my friend, Jesus did not come so that we would have to continue to try and please God ourselves. He came so that He could do it for us, and give it to us as a gift. That's why the Word (who is Jesus) directs us on how we are to live in Him with our minds set on Him and His ways. I tell you what, let's look at what the Word says here:

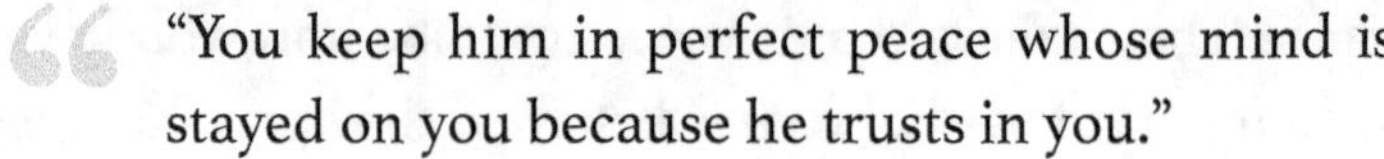

> "You keep him in perfect peace whose mind is stayed on you because he trusts in you."
>
> Isaiah 26:3

> "For to set the mind on the flesh is death, but to set the mind on the Spirit is life and peace."
>
> Romans 8:6

So if the mind set on the flesh is bad, how do we get free? We receive the good news. Believe that you are not under the law any longer because of what Jesus did for us. Receive His covenant of Grace. The flesh is hostile because it wants what it wants and always will. It doesn't want God or you interfering with what makes it feel good. It's a sin nature. "Don't tell me what to do!" That's why the cross deals with the sinner. The person is born of a sinful nature. The blood dealt with our sins, but the cross dealt with the sinner. This is why we were crucified with Christ and resurrected with Him, so we can have the mind of Christ! Having the mind of Christ is not something that we can do ourselves. The Word of God washes and renews our minds supernaturally. But until we receive Jesus as more than just our way to heaven, and realize, accept, and believe that He is our new covenant, Grace, we won't allow Him to do in us what He has already done and prepared for us. It's also why we have to substantiate that we were in Truth, crucified and it's no longer us that lives, but Christ that lives in us, and the life we live in the flesh we live through Christ. His power, His ability, His goodness! His promises! He is our covenant of Grace and we have to substantiate it's His life in us. Christ in us is the hope of glory! He justified us and He also glorified us. By being in us! We have to know and believe right so that the life we now live in the flesh, we live through the Son of God. All that He did for us, He does in us and as we believe all His Word tells us rightly dividing law from Grace, we will live the life we preach we're supposed to have. You will have that!

I was talking to my 19-year-old son who was home on Christmas break from Christ for the Nations, a Bible college in Dallas, TX. He was telling me about some things someone told him at church that morning. He said, "I don't get it, it's like they are trying to sound like they have some great spiritual secret and they just keep talking about like all this stuff to make themselves sound like they are just so spiritual, talking about missing books from the Bible and secrets God has told them and it's like where's Jesus in all that?" He said, "Dad, it's just like Paul said," and opened his Bible app to read me 1 Corinthians 2:2. Praise God! My son gets it! When we have a revelation of who Jesus is, and receive the covenant of His blood, when we understand all that Grace did for us. We will declare as Paul did, I have decided to know nothing among you except Him crucified. Our conversation is different when our mind is set on Jesus, we think differently because Grace gives us the mind of Christ. Law will always give us an anti-Grace mind, and Grace will always give us the mind of Christ.

TEN

Armored identity

"Finally, be strong in the Lord and in the strength of his might. Put on the whole armor of God, so that you may be able to stand against the schemes of the devil. For we do not wrestle against flesh and blood, but against the rulers, against the authorities, against the cosmic powers over this present darkness, against the spiritual forces of evil in the heavenly places. Therefore take up the whole armor of God, that you may be able to withstand in the evil day, and having done all, to stand firm. Stand therefore, having fastened on the belt of truth, and having put on the breastplate of righteousness, and, as shoes for your feet, having put on the readiness given by the gospel of peace. In all circumstances take up the shield of faith, with which you can extinguish all the flaming darts of the evil one; and take the helmet of salvation, and the sword of the Spirit,

> which is the word of God, praying at all times in the Spirit, with all prayer and supplication. To that end, keep alert with all perseverance, making supplication for all the saints,"
>
> Ephesians 6:10-18 ESV

THIS MAY BE the most important chapter of this book!

"Why do you say that pastor?" I say that, because this passage of scripture has been one of the most underrated, misunderstood, and even used out of context to fit a doctrinal narrative, of any scripture passage in the Bible in my opinion. We have made this one of our "spiritual warfare" mantras. We have seen it preached like a pep talk before a battle to rev up the troops and get them stirred up to fight the enemy. It's been quoted as prayer guides in the context of being ready to take the fight to the enemy in our day. To take back what he stole from us, to emotionally draw us into a mindset of doing battle with the devil. We have books written on this passage breaking down each of the various parts of armor and how to use each piece in battle. Can I ask you a question? How's that working for you so far? How many of you get up every morning and in your prayer time put on your armor so you can kick the devil in the teeth safely without him being able to hit you back? Only to realize on your morning commute when that car cut you off that you somehow left it back at the house? LOL. Come on you know what I am talking about. That car cut you off or honked at you, the slow driver in the fast lane, and suddenly the thoughts that come and the words that jump out of our mouth immediately show us that we do not have our helmet on and who knows where we left the sword of the Spirit which is the Word of God!! Because those thoughts and words do not testify of our salvation and they certainly are not from the Word of God! What happened? How could this be? You prayed your Amor of God prayer guide like you do every morning. Most of us would probably say "I don't know, I don't understand why I do that! I guess I just got in the flesh!"Then the enemy comes with the accusations and condemnation. "Thought you were a Christian? You can't even act right for five minutes!" "You blew it now! God is not happy with you now." And on and on. This has been case after case for so many believers that I have talked to over the last 30 years in ministry. I believe the answer to the question is that we do not understand this passage because it is mixed with law almost every time it has been taught! Let me show you what I mean.

Every time I ever heard this taught growing up, the *responsibility was on me to put on the armor.* The pastor would say something like, "Take up your shield of faith! You have to get that shield! That shield is your faith. If you don't have faith you are not going to win against the enemy and you cannot please God without faith!" I would hear, "Your feet shod with the preparation of the gospel of peace! If you don't have peace you need to get some peace from the Lord! He is the Prince of Peace and you need to pray it through until you have peace!" Does any of that sound familiar? Yes pastor that's similar to the way I heard it! What's wrong with that? I am glad you asked. Let's break this down just a little bit and talk Bible.

Faith, where does it come from? The Bible says Jesus is the author and perfecter of our faith. The Bible says that to each man who believes, a measure of faith is given. It is a gift from Jesus who authored it and will perfect it in us! So it cannot be my responsibility to achieve faith. I only need to receive it as a gift and say thank you, Jesus! If I could take up faith for myself, I wouldn't need Jesus. Next, any time someone starts talking about if you don't do this, then the enemy will win, they are bringing the law and its ways back into your life. The enemy is a defeated foe. Jesus disarmed the enemy and made a spectacle out of them. So the only things the enemy has to try and come at us with are lies and confusion. The lie being the accusations from the stance of the law and/or the law mixed with Grace. Either way it brings a veil so that the people don't understand the truth. Then the enemy brings the confusion because the people cannot understand the Truth. It's the why, in all the times we prayed the armor of God prayers, putting on the armor ourselves in our attempt to understand what it was and how it worked, and then it didn't work. You see? Its like someone without a pilot license trying to fly a plane. You can try, but on your own your going to crash The truth is, we can't put the armor on ourselves first of all. Secondly, the armor is not for us to be able to fight the enemy at work in our lives! "Pastor, you're going to have to explain what you're talking about here because the verse says Put on!" You're right, let me explain. It might be helpful to look at the original Greek here! The Greek word here is the word "Endusasthe". It means to clothe or be clothed with (in the sense of sinking into a garment). Picture yourself melding into a new suit or dress. The look, the feel, the swag! You know what I am talking about. You get dressed up in your garments, your new outfit, you just "wear it". Throw some swag on, a little touch of bling maybe, and suddenly you look the part. You become the look. It's what people will identify you by if someone asks, what did you look like? Paul was using this metaphor of the armor taken from how the Roman centurion looked with all their outfit on ready to make their stand against any enemy. Another point to make here, the Roman army never went out to pick a fight or start a war. They went to occupy the land. To them any land they desired to occupy was theirs and anyone who would oppose them became the enemy. The Romans simply showed up in full force and declared the land was now theirs. If another army came against them, the Roman army just stood its ground. When the enemy that came at them was defeated, they would advance taking more ground. Of course in the natural the Roman armies fought and killed the enemy. But Paul understood the tactical approach of how the Romans would just go where they were sent and declare the land their own. Then stand! The armor and shield along with their swords identified them as Roman soldiers and it was who they were. He used this to drive home the point that we do have an enemy out there in the spiritual realm that wants to kill, steal, and destroy our lives, the Lord has placed us or sent us to occupy a region and the enemy wants to keep what he stole, but he can only do that if we are not equipped with the identity Jesus has given us. But it's important to understand this whole context so let's keep going. So we "endusasthe" the whole armor, which sounds more like accepting an identity, than dressing up. Melding into this identity is exactly what Jesus had in mind when He gave us these gifts to receive. He wants us to look like Him! And when we receive these gifts, when we believe we are, these very things in Christ, we take on His identity, and our identity roots in and is changed to be His. He gives us the identity, the pieces that make up our identity He puts in our lives as we receive them, He does the change in us.

Let's look at each of these gifts. The helmet of salvation. Salvation is a gift from Jesus! Paul says helmet because when receive this gift from Jesus by Grace, through faith in Him, Christ is the head of the church, He is the crown, He is King, and Salvation is found only in the Head. It made sense for salvation to be the "helmet" on the head. It's interesting though that Paul starts with the belt of Truth. Truth is a person, Truth is Jesus. He declared In John 14 that He is the Truth. Paul equates Truth with the belt because the belt in the centurion's wardrobe held everything together. I tell you what, let's break it all down in this chapter starting from the beginning of Ephesians 6:10.

Put on - Greek word "endusasthe" as mentioned above, which means to clothe or be clothed with (in the sense of sinking into a garment or meld into); comes from the root word "dunō", which means to enter, to sink into. This sense of sinking into, or to meld into infers to become unified with or as one. When we look at the gifts Jesus has purchased for us, even as Paul is using the Roman centurion armor as the metaphor, there is a strong inference of becoming one with these gifts, as we believe they are who we are in Christ. They are the gifts that Jesus gave to us that we exchange our identities for. We become, or meld into these gifts. This reminds me of when we would gear up for SWAT. You had spent a lot of time getting the gear rightly set for your body. Your size, shape everything mattered or it didn't fit right. When you are about to face an enemy, you want your gear to feel as though it is just a part of you. Your weapon is an extension of you, but your armor becomes a part of who you are. It moves with you and after a while, you don't even realize it's there until the battle comes and it protects you from a blow from the enemy. Then you remember, you have this armor and you can stand your ground and press the fight! Of course in the spiritual realm Jesus already won the fight, so we just stand, resting in Him and all He has done, and this armor He has given us is ours to stand and not be moved by the lies of the enemy.

It's not an accident that Paul starts with the Truth, and it wasn't by chance that he chose to use the belt as the metaphor for Truth. We have to know the Truth. Truth is the Word who became flesh (Jesus) and came and dwelt among us. So the depth of this is this, we become one with the Truth. And we must accurately divide the Word of God. The old covenant and new covenant do not mix. The Bible says the new has replaced the old. So as we learn His Word we are learning Jesus, we become one with the Truth. When that happens the Truth sets you free. So the Truth becomes our identity. When we walk in the Truth, as part of who we are in Christ, then everything else in that makes up our identity connects through Jesus. Since we have established He is the Truth, then anything else will not do. The next thing Paul lists as a gift from Jesus is righteousness. He uses the metaphor of the breastplate for this. Again, not an accident. The Bible says that His righteousness is a gift from Jesus. Paul likens it to the breastplate probably because it was the part that protected the abdomen. When we look at the spiritual significance of this, the spirit of a man is in his abdomen. We know this from scripture references. One in particular Jesus prophesied that whoever believed in Him would have rivers of living water flowing out of his belly (John 7:38). I would think that is a pretty important part, how about you? When we know and believe we are His righteousness, then nothing the enemy can throw at us can penetrate our spirit. It's just who we are in Him. The lies of condemnation, guilt and shame don't get past the truth we are His righteousness. We are in Christ forever in right standing with God! Therefore, there is now no condemnation in Christ. Because of His gift of righteousness! We will talk more about this down a little further. But let's jump to the helmet.

Helmet of Salvation Greek word soteria meaning Deliverance from our enemies, all evils, sickness and disease, fear and depression... whatever attack the enemy tries to bring, Jesus has provided Deliverance through Him. It would also make sense that it's the helmet that protects the head that Paul chooses as the "Soteria". It all starts with how we think, and how we believe. Right believing, when we know the Truth when we know that Jesus came to fulfill the old law and bring a new covenant of Grace, and that the two do not go together. When we know that even God put the stone tablets of law away inside the ark of the covenant, and then put the mercy seat on top of it symbolizing that Jesus would put away the old law and mercy would triumph over judgment. When we believe we have the mind of Christ because of the finished work of the cross and through Christ living in us we have access to all the promises and more in Him. When we believe all has been done for us. He has prepared a table for us in the presence of our enemy. That we are seated in heavenly places with Christ and that in Him we reign with Christ on the earth. When we believe right, we will live right! It all starts with how we believe. Smith Wigglesworth used to say "only believe" as he opened up the time of healing in his meetings. If you believe Jesus will heal you and you believe you can receive that now, then as Jesus told almost every person that He healed, your faith in this Truth has made make you well. The Bible says the prayer of faith **will** make the sick person well! Notice it doesn't say could or might. It says it will. The key is right believing. Faith in Jesus! This is also why the enemy comes and attacks our thought life. When the enemy throws the "fiery darts" they are just lies. It's the only weapon he has. He was disarmed, so therefore, he only has lies. He knows that if we don't rightly believe, or do not know Truth, then his lies will deceive us into believing anything else but Truth. The only spiritual battle there is for the believer, is the battle for the mind! For right believing and knowledge of Truth and Life!

Truth and Life are the only things God wanted us to have. Remember God told Adam not to eat of the Tree of the knowledge of ***good*** and evil. God didn't want us to know anything but Him! Even Jesus said "why do you call me good? Only the Father is good." If the enemy can just get us to believe that something good is of God then he can deceive us and we will miss what God intended. But Jesus gave us soteria! So when we receive it all and rightly believe that we are, then we walk in faith as who He is!

The Greek manuscript of Hebrews 11:1 says that faith is the substantiating or assuring of things hoped for and the conviction that it is already while not being seen. The definition of substantiate is to uphold as though it is actual substance. The definition of assurance is to confidently dispel any doubt. Now how many of us receive healing upholding that it is done, that it has become the substance of our body, confidently going on as though there is no doubt that we are completely healed. That is called faith! When we believe that we are healed and receive the free gift of healing from Jesus as an actual substance with no doubt, we are healed. Notice that nowhere does it mention how we feel. That's because it doesn't have anything to do with how we feel. It has to do with faith in Jesus and believing His body was broken for our healing. That by His stripes we are healed. He purchased our healing and therefore we can receive it. He purchased our Joy so we can have it. Live in it! He purchased our freedom from fear, depression, and oppression from evil or unclean spirits, so in Him we can have this abundant life He came to give us. So salvation is so much more than being saved from an eternal death separated from God, He came to save us from the law of sin and death. He came to save us from sickness, disease, and every evil thing. When we know and believe this Truth, we can rightly receive all the other gifts and promises from the Lord.

Shoes of the Gospel of Peace... crushing Peace... Roman 16:20 says the God of Peace will soon crush satan underneath your feet. Peace is depicted as the shoes here, but in Greek, it's contextually more about our footing position in Peace. The Peace we stand in is crushing to the enemy because when we walk in or stand in His Peace we can withstand the lies of fear and anxiety and the enemy cannot steal our Joy. When we accept and receive Him as our covenant of Grace knowing all that Grace has done for us, it brings His Peace that surpasses all understanding and it guards our hearts and minds. It's a position of standing in Him that brings peace that we can't explain to others at times.

I remember when I was a police officer. We had an incident where I was shot at with an AK-47. The bullet passed by my head with such force that I felt the compression hit me in the chest. I remember as I ducked for cover behind my vehicle looking down and feeling my chest to make sure that I had not been hit. The incident lasted almost an hour as other officers arrived on the scene. We took the shooter into custody without firing a shot. The uniformed officer who was originally at the scene with me later said he thought for sure I had been shot. He immediately turned for cover in his car and began yelling officer down shots fired into the radio. Which brought officers from all over the area to assist. Numerous officers and supervisors asked me, "Are you ok? Are you good? You sure?" Even days later I would be stopped in the hall and asked how I was doing. We had a debriefing meeting and I was offered to take time if I needed it to talk to the department shrink and rest up. To all of it, I would just smile and tell them, no, thank you I am good. And I was good. I had a peace that didn't make sense to many. I wasn't moved because I was not afraid and my Peace is not of this world. For many years when I have heard people describe me, peace is always one of the attributes they list. I am thankful to Jesus for His Peace that I stand in. My friend this is a position you too can stand in and not be moved no matter what the circumstance is. Maybe you struggle with fear or anxiousness, and people have prayed and rebuked fear and anxiety off your life and you try your hardest to believe it is gone! But then it's just suddenly there. Can I suggest to you that it's not about the prayer of people rebuking the fear? I'm sure if there is an evil spirit trying to oppress you with fear, it goes away when they pray. But why does it so easily return just hours later, or days later? It's about right believing! It's an identity issue, that you haven't fully received the armored gifts of Grace, or moreover you don't realize what the gifts do in your life. These shoes of preparation for the gospel of peace, mean that you can and have the right to stand in His Peace and when we receive that as Truth, then we stand immovable by the lies of the enemy, or even by our feelings.

A Peace that surpasses all understanding. Believe it and receive it!

Shield of faith! Interestingly, Paul uses the Roman shield as the metaphor for faith here because the shields were really large! They could protect two people. The soldier carrying it and the man next to it if needed. In certain tactical formations the shields were locked together in front and above the soldiers to form what was called the testudo formation, sometimes referred to as the tortoise formation, because the soldiers were almost completely protected from the arrows of the enemy that could come from in front of them or from above them. What about the rear guard? Glad you asked... we have a rear guard, the Bible says that God is our rear God! (Jesus does not allow the enemy to come up behind you sight unseen. He by His Spirit protects our back! (Isaiah 52) But I never saw it coming. We will talk about where your eyes were later. But the shield of faith is large and covers fully. The Bible says that it stops all the fiery darts of the enemy. Did you know that the Greek word for darts in this scripture is the word "belos". Which means a missile, dart, javelin, or arrow. I think it is interesting that the modern-day weapon of missiles has been added as the technology of weapons in the natural have developed. It adds a more emphasized faith.

In other words, the shield of faith can stop anything the enemy throws at us. And the best part to me is that anything the enemy throws at us is a lie. Jesus is Truth, so therefore anything the enemy brings is a lie and therefore subject to the shield of faith. Pastor, what do you mean anything he throws is a lie? Well aside from the fact that the Bible says he is the father of lies, and author of confusion, the Bible also says he is defeated already. More importantly, he has been disarmed according to the Bible. The fact that his name means accuser, he is only ever able to bring accusations of sin to try to put us under the law! The fact that Jesus disarmed him by putting away his law, and made a spectacle out of them the Bible says, further demonstrates that the enemy is powerless! So why do so many preachers and ministries still teach and preach spiritual warfare and that we have to fight the enemy if we want to be victorious in Jesus? Does that even make sense? It would only make sense if we believed that Jesus was victorious but we are not yet. But the Truth is, that in Christ we are more than conquerors, we are victorious and we have all authority in heaven and earth through Him!

The armor is not so we can fight a battle that Jesus already won. It says, so that we can withstand the enemy. It says that so that we can stand immovable in Christ. We have a position in Christ and when we live by faith in the Son of God, and we receive sonship and rightly believe we are who He says we are in Him, living by His Spirit, then by faith we pull down every argument and thought that exalts itself against the knowledge of God, our faith is our shield that when the enemy comes with his lies, and oppression, sickness or disease, evil or unclean spirits, and we declare in authority he may not trespass against the temple of the Holy Spirit. We declare the Word and the enemy's assault does not prosper. No weapon formed, no lie, no sickness, no oppression, nothing the enemy forms against a son or daughter of God shall prosper. That is the Truth. Are you seeing how Truth connects it all?

The Truth holds all of it together. Because it is all in Him, He is Himself all of it! He is the Word, He is Grace and Truth, He is... So it is all found in Him, a life surrendered to Him.

When we say here is my life, Lord, it's yours and we truly mean it, truly surrendered, we have been born again into Christ. So it's His life to live through us. Where we miss it a lot in understanding Grace, is the word freedom, or free. We declare we are free! It's not free to live however you want to. It's not freedom to live how we want at all. It's in Christ we are free from the law of sin and death. We are free from the slavery of sin! Free from the enemy's rule of this earth, free from darkness. Born into this wonderful Light! Jesus Christ. We receive that freedom through our surrender to Him. We are crucified with Christ and it is no longer us that lives, but Christ that lives in us, and this life in the flesh we live through Him. What does through Him mean? It means, "Jesus, what do you want me to do? Jesus how do you want me to act, Jesus you show me, Jesus you lead me, Jesus I am Yours! Lead me by Your Spirit. It's walking in the Spirit and not in the flesh. It's walking with all our faith in Jesus. The Roman armor, the belt, which was more like a girdle, connected to the boots, the breastplate, and the helmet. It would cinch up the armor so that the parts were all secured. When we know the Truth, we can apply Truth and Truth sets us free. Moreover, we become the vessel of Truth to share it with the world. It's who we are in Christ. Going back to my days as a police officer, it was ingrained in us from the days of the academy, that police officers should be people who know and tell the truth. It's in the code of ethics we had to memorize and recite daily at the academy and finished our graduation ceremony by reciting it as a class. In the code of ethics, it says, "Honest in thought and deed..." It was to be who we are as police officers. Now I learned quickly that not every police officer lives the code of ethics. But like it, being people of Truth, means we are to live a life worthy. We cannot do that in our own effort. Only Grace can produce that in us. When we contend with this flesh through Jesus rather than our efforts, then Grace and Truth are revealed to those around us. People begin to see that we are people of Truth and trustworthiness. I have people who will call me or my wife and ask us for Biblical counsel. They say, "Well I called you because I knew you would tell me the truth!" What a compliment that glorifies Jesus! What He has done in our lives, people see and they trust us to tell them the truth. We have also known people who stopped coming around us for a while. When we would finally see them again, they would admit, "Well I stopped coming around because I knew you would tell me the truth and I didn't want to hear at that time!" We are thankful they finally repented and came back around and they are also greeted with love and acceptance. It's the Truth in our lives that allows us to declare the Truth to the world. It's also knowing the Truth that holds all the other gifts in their proper place securely in Truth. The truth is He is our salvation (Soteria), He is our gift of Righteousness, He is our Peace, He gives us faith, He is the Word and He alone is Truth. In Him so too are we. The Bible says, as He is so are we in the earth.

The Breastplate of Righteousness stops the enemies' assault on our hearts and spirits. There is no harder impact in a believer's life than to believe the lie that God is mad at us. That we have blown it with God and that He is just waiting to hurl a giant lightning bolt of judgment at us. We have been taught in churches that when we sin, bad things are going to happen until we repent and ask God to forgive us. We have heard it preached that sometimes God puts sickness on people to teach them a lesson. We have heard that God is sovereign and does not change, so when we sin his wrath is being stored up against us. We have heard sinners in the hands of an angry God! We have heard so much law preached and then the feel-good leverage of Grace to get people to an altar comes just at the end. We have heard give your tithes or you will be cursed. Not realizing that when we hold to this covenant of law we are in fact under bondage. So many laws that when the breastplate of righteousness is talked about, it comes out like decoration of armor, which is the furthest thing from the Truth. So here it is my friend. The Breastplate of Righteousness is the last line of defense! In the armor of the Roman centurion, the breastplate was there because, in battle, the soldier could not always have his shield defending every blow of the enemy. The breastplate protects the most important part of the body. The heart and abdomen. So if the soldier was blocking a blow with his shield, and the enemy saw an opening to the vital area and took it, the breastplate protected the soldier. When our identity in Christ is solidified as His Righteousness, no matter what we are facing, what the enemy is throwing at us, knowing we are His righteousness, knowing that we are in Right Standing with our Father God through Jesus, means we can always run to Him, retreat into Him, even if we mess up. God cannot be mad at His Righteousness. The Bible says that God sees us Righteous because of Jesus when He looks at us. That means that we can boldly come into His Throne Room and receive help in our time of need. Let's remember why He sees His righteousness. All sin forever was judged at the cross on Jesus. So even if it feels like we have lost our faith, even if it feels like we have dropped our sword, if the circumstances have been so terrible and we have made the wrong choices, and when we have been knocked down from our position of peace. We are still His righteousness and we are being renewed day by day. No matter what the enemy or this life throws at us when we rightly believe we are His righteousness, we are in Him, and He is in us, we may be knocked down but we are not destroyed. We get up for His mercy is new every morning, and we stand again in Christ because "greater is He that is in us than he that is in this world ".. Knowing God is not mad at us, knowing that He loves us beyond comprehension, knowing that He blesses us because of His goodness, and not because of our efforts! He can't help but bless us when He sees us in right standing through Christ. He just sees His children. He withholds no good thing. Don't let the enemy strip you of your identity of Righteousness. When we begin to believe the lies of condemnation, guilt, and shame, we are allowing the enemy to talk us into removing that breastplate. When we do that, we give him access to our spirit and our heart. He will sow the lies of condemnation into our hearts and we begin to speak in alignment with those lies. When we find ourselves speaking what the enemy has sown, we know there is an identity issue. The breastplate of righteousness has been taken off and we have forgotten who we are in Christ. Then we begin to speak from the abundance of the heart, from how we feel and we get caught up in a life of guilt and shame, depression sets in as we become oppressed by the enemy who is trying to steal kill, and destroy us. Don't fall into that trap! When the enemy comes and tries to put you under condemnation, the breastplate of Righteousness guards against those lies. We are His. No matter what choices, no matter what we have done, He is our Righteousness! For clarification only, this is not a license to live a sinful life! When we truly believe all that Jesus has done and submit ourselves under Grace, Grace produces holiness in us. Grace produces obedience to the leading of the Spirit of God. Those that are led by the Spirit of God are sons and daughters of God. So remember you are His Righteousness.

The Sword of the Spirit is the Word of God. It proceeds from His mouth and so it should from ours. When the enemy throws lies at us or others in our lives, the Spirit reminds of us His Word and as we declare the Word, the Truth cuts off the lies and routes the enemy. The beautiful poetic part of this illustration is that Jesus is the Word! So many times, like you I am sure, I have heard this taught as though we were to wield the word as our sword in fighting the enemy! Many have even included, using the Word to debate and argue with each other. Which is not Biblical either. When you think about Jesus is the Word, which is the sword of the Spirit. Then we see clearly that in any situation we declare Jesus and all He is. When the enemy or a circumstance in life, or even a mixture of both present themselves in our lives, we simply declare Jesus. Is it sickness? Jesus heals. Is it a financial matter? Jesus is provision. No matter what it is, the name of Jesus is above it all. When the enemy comes with shame or guilt, Jesus already forgave and cleansed us with His blood. The answer is the Word. The Word is Jesus. Speak Jesus. When we bind and loose in the spiritual realm in the name of Jesus, things are bound and loose. When we ask the Father in Jesus name according to His will it shall be done. So the enemy stops, ceases, and flees in the name of Jesus. When we pull out the "Sword" the Word. The enemy stops, ceases, and flees! We resist him with Jesus and he flees. I want to challenge you with this, know the Word. Not because David hid it in his heart that he might not sin against God, but because He loves us and to [know] (the Greek word "Ginōskō" - to know intimately) the Word is to know His character and covenant for us. To know Him intimately changes us, as He is in us, the Bible says as He is so are we on the earth. As sons and daughters of God, the Word is alive in us by His Spirit. When we speak the "sword" the enemy flees. He doesn't fight, he flees.

The 7th part of the armor is not like the rest. Notice Paul ends the description with pray in the Spirit at all times and on all occasions. I spent 7 years in fulltime law enforcement. Three of those years on SWAT. You might say pastor that 7 years isn't that long, and you would be right in comparison to those who served 15, 20 even 30 years in law enforcement. But that's irrelevant to the point I want to make here. I learned a lot in law enforcement. But one of the things I want to tell you about really drives home Paul's statement of "pray in the Spirit at all times." You see communication in law enforcement is your lifeline. What a lot of people don't know is that during an incident where an officer is deployed to, or even multiple officers, the agency's communication center (often referred to as "dispatch") is constantly checking on the officers. The officers are talking to dispatch for various informational reasons. The officers are also always communicating with each other. Whether over the radio or in person verbal and non-verbal communication is constantly happening. During my days on SWAT, there was even more communication required between us operators as we moved through an incident. Something we trained during all training was verbal and non-verbal communication. When clearing a structure, communication was vital. If you were moving to do anything, you communicated with your teammates that you were moving. If two dumped into a room to clear it, you would often hear, "Cover! Covering! Moving! Clear!" From the two operators clearing. When they had both determined the room clear, both would announce "clear" and one or both would then state, "Room clear! Two coming out!" So that the other operators in the stack outside the room would know the room was clear and two teammates were ready to exit the room. They waited however until they heard "come out" from one of the other operators. This level of communication was done under the stress of training so that when we were dispatched to a live incident we would do what we trained. Communicate constantly. The enemy was real, we needed to be in constant communication with each other. If SWAT was deployed a special command center was also set up at or near the scene. Referred to as Tactical Operations Command or "TOC", this is who the team leaders were in communication with as well, receiving orders on when to breach or hold, etc. The operators heard from TOC before anything was done.

So in the big picture of life and following Jesus in our every direction, it makes complete sense that Paul would include talking to the Lord constantly as part of the armor metaphor. It's who we should be! People who are in constant communication with the Lord. And if we don't know what to say or how to pray, the Bible says that the Holy Spirit will pray through us. I think that's why Paul also said he thanked God that he was able to pray in tongues more than the rest. Grace and Truth have given us this identity in Him that Paul has broken down into a wonderful metaphor of armor, because when our identity is solid in these areas as we are in Christ, then we can with all authority stand against the enemy when he comes to try and start a fight. We can rest in His peace knowing who we are in Him and the Truth that the enemy has been disarmed and he is a liar. So we have this joy and peace because we are His righteousness. And Jesus declared that the Kingdom of God is righteousness, peace, and joy in the Holy Spirit. So I want to encourage you today to let the striving cease. Stop looking at all the enemy is trying to do through the circumstances of life, and stop listening to the lies of the enemy. Turn your eyes to Jesus and meld into your identity in Him. All that He has done and given to us. As you do, you will watch as the enemy begins to back down and fade from view. Truth and Grace always call the enemy's bluff! Stand in the power of His might fully clothed in His identity that is rightfully ours because of Jesus.

ELEVEN

Crushing Grace

I HAVE HEARD SO MUCH of the Christianese talk about the crushing. "If you want the new wine you have to go through the crushing". To be honest, I have preached it before myself! It can be easy to draw these conclusions from the various places in the Bible that talk about the crushing, while we are going through difficult times. It's like as pastors, we can just give out hope, if we just tell the people that the crushing they're going through is not for nothing then we will have helped! That God uses the crushing to make us stronger or to teach us something. I heard that a lot growing up. The pressing, the crushing it's going to bring new wine in us. And we will be better spiritually for it. But once again my friend, I must declare to you, that is all wrong. Not the crushed part per se, because we all know we go through difficult times. In this world we will have "trials and tribulations", this is what Jesus told us, but then he immediately said, "But fear not, for I have overcome the world." It's interesting that He said that before He went to the cross. Like so many times in the first four books of the New Testament, Jesus is speaking prophetically concerning who He is, what He is going to do and what He has done. The issue here is that so many have taken the trials and tribulations of this world and made it a requirement for growth. They have put a spin on it to explain away in defense of God why bad things happen. It's a fact that we do often gain wisdom or learn through the difficult times. It also truth that God can and often does turn those things around for our good, but He didn't put them on us in order to teach us something. The hardest truth in the Bible sometimes to explain is why bad things happen to good people. But when we begin to make it about something God is doing in our lives, we end up crushing Grace and Truth.

What is the truth about going through difficult times? The truth is, we will go through trials and difficult circumstances because we live in a fallen world that has a prince of darkness named satan, whose entire goal is to kill steal, and destroy. We will face hard times because of the sinful nature of men. This world and all its possessions are headed for destruction and sinful men will make choices that will cause others pain and grief. This is not a "process" that we must go through to become more spiritual or to become closer to Jesus or more like Jesus. It is not a requirement that we go through a difficult time or sinful struggle to be qualified to preach or teach about it. Going through a "crushing" time in life, we often do tend to cry out to the Lord and so we should. He is the fourth man in the fires of life. But we have to be honest with ourselves. Never will the Holy Spirit lead us into a crushing circumstance of His own doing. The hard truth here is we often find ourselves in situations of our own choices. If that is not the case, then we are sometimes forced into crushing moments because of other's decisions. Then there are those times when difficult times just come. Perhaps a violent storm devastates, or an earthquake shatters, or a disease like cancer shows up. It is no one's fault. None of these crushing moments are brought into our lives by God to bring us closer to Him, although we often run to God when they show up. He didn't do anything, If we want to backtrack the origin of why bad things happen, we can blame Adam. It was by Adam that sin entered the world and the sinful nature of humans has caused us to be where we are today. But through Jesus, the "last man", we now have access to ever-present help in times of trouble. Because He is with us in the storm, moreover, He walks in the storms of life. Moreover, He now lives in us by His Spirit dwelling in us! Through His new covenant of Grace, we now have access to the Father who gives good gifts to His children, not because we completed a crushing moment in life, but simply because He is a good Father! He looks at us in our cry for help and sees His righteousness. He can't help but help. We have to put away this mixing of law and Grace and believe that amid the storm we now have the authority to speak to the storm. Peace be still! We have a table prepared for us that has all we need in Christ. When bad things happen, the enemy likes to immediately come with accusations and condemnation to move us from our position in Christ back under the law. It's all he has. Lies and condemnation in hopes that we are not firmly rooted in Christ's identity and he can somehow get us back on the path of destruction through it. So he will come as light and declare that the crushing is required to be more spiritual. Then when we don't feel more spiritual, he immediately comes with condemnation. The Truth is, we cannot be more spiritual than the Holy Spirit. He is in us as believers who received Him. We will never be more spiritual than Him. We will, however, experience encounters with Him that are tangible and we feel those moments and we feel His presence and connect on a spiritual level where we feel Him close to us in those moments.

The problem comes when we don't "feel" spiritual on Monday at work when the circumstances are different, or worse we get let go. We have become so accustomed to getting the feel at church or a meeting, and then we go home and because someone preached or wrote a book on the crushing, when Monday hit, we immediately line up with the crushing as something the Lord is doing to grow us. When the Truth is we should simply ask Jesus what's next. When we remember His covenant of Grace and know that He didn't bring the hardship, but that He is the answer to the hardship, then we can walk through the difficult moment or "crushing" in the power of His might and release faith in Him by looking to Him for the answer. If we instead of reacting in our flesh abilities and allowing worry and fear in about how we will pay the bills, sit down at the table He prepared, not having been moved from our stance of Peace, and just ask Him what to do, He will lead us by His Spirit to the next place. What about when we do ask and He doesn't answer immediately? Keep asking! It's okay to be the Child of God. When I first resigned from law enforcement, we packed up our family and moved to a small town. I took a part-time job to just make the rent and overhead. But things didn't seem to be moving forward like we thought. The offer from a pastor friend wasn't panning out. I began to fast and pray. I told my wife I am going to fast and talk to the Lord because we need an answer here! I was doing my best not to allow worry in. I was also doing my best to hold it together as the priest of my home. On day three of the fast I was out walking in the woods around our rented house. I was telling the Father all the issues. I was telling Him that I needed to know what was next and what He wanted us to do. I will never forget His answer to me for the rest of my life! When I finally stopped whining to Him, I heard Him almost audibly, it was just a clear and gentle loud voice in my spirit. He said something profound. He said, "Hold on a minute! I am doing something here!" Immediately a peace that surpassed all understanding washed over me. As a child who finally got a reply from his Father, would remember, "Oh yeah I knew you had it taken care of" and would just feel a little humbled, and yet it brought a stabilizing calm, I just smiled and said thank you, Jesus. Thank you, Father.

I knew immediately I didn't need to continue fasting and begging God to show me. He was already taking care of it. He was at work! So don't be afraid to keep going to the Lord until He answers. He will answer. Make sure you give Him the opportunity. That means at some point we should shut up and just listen. No matter what we go through, know this with all confidence. Jesus didn't cause it. Don't let the law crush Grace in your life. Jesus is the answer and we can trust in Him and the finished work of the cross to bring us through. When we prevent law from crushing Grace by separating law from Grace, we flip the script on the plans of the enemy!

"For I am not ashamed of this Good News about Christ. It is the power of God at work, saving

> everyone who believes—the Jew first and also the Gentile."
>
> Romans 1:16 NLT

Paul makes it abundantly clear that the Good News of Jesus, which is a lot, is the power of God working. Grace is the Good News! Think about it for a minute. If someone came up to you and said, "Hey I have some Good News about Jesus!" You would reply with some form of the question, "What is it?" What's the good news? The good news is not just that Jesus died on the cross for your sins. Don't give me that "old-time religion" that the message of Jesus dying on the cross for our sins is the only "good news". No one is going to understand that.

"So, the good news about Jesus is that He is the Messiah and He died on the cross so you can be forgiven of your sins! Yeah!" Huh? Ok, thanks, man! First of all who is the "Messiah"? Secondly, why would someone die for me? I have done way too much wrong to be forgiven. Then we have to bring in the whole church and Bible thing and that's where they check out and immediately go to the default, "Oh you're a religious person trying to convert me." But pastor. isn't Jesus dying on the cross for our sins the good news? Technically, it's more like pulling one chapter out of the book of "good news" and claiming that the chapter is the only good news. And then let's stand on the four gospels of Jesus and teach everyone who Jesus was and is and then mix YHWH in there with Moses and the Ten Commandments, and Levitical laws, and Hosea's wife and the prophet Joel and Samuel, then take them straight to Revelations and the throne room of God with creatures covered in eyes circling the throne with 24 elders falling down in worship, while adamantly and fervently preaching how God hates our sin and we could never be in His presence without first getting right with God by always making sure we seek His forgiveness, especially if we want to participate in communion without the risk of getting weak or sick or even dying before our time because we didn't get right with God so we took the communion in an unworthy manner! OMG! Is anyone else ready to throw in the towel here? Where is the Good News already? Because I caught something about Jesus dying so I can be forgiven, but there is no way I can live the Ten Commandments. That isn't good news!

You see my friend if we don't understand that the new covenant of His blood, Grace, and all that included for us and that we are no longer UNDER the law, which includes the Ten Commandments, which includes seeking forgiveness constantly for sins because the Bible declares that ALL sin, forever, has been judged at that cross and the blood of Jesus paid one time and it will forever be enough. When we don't realize that the old covenant has been replaced forever by Jesus' covenant of Grace, then we allow the enemy to bring the crushing condemnation into our lives. But when we know the Truth that came, that Truth in us sets us free! Then Grace begins to crush the lies of the enemy in our lives. Grace begins to crush the ways of our flesh, Grace begins to produce holiness in us and as we are separated ***to God***, Grace produces obedience in us. The old law required obedience, a requirement that our flesh was at odds with. The new covenant of Grace produces obedience in us. We love Him because He loved us first, so we delight ourselves in Him and He puts His desires in our hearts! Furthermore, the Bible says that in Christ, we uphold the law. It is not us doing it it is Christ in us who upheld and met the righteous requirements of the law, therefore in Him, we are credited as having done the same. So that is why the Bible says, "Those He justified, He also glorified!" When we know the Truth, we know that we receive Him apart from the law, apart from our efforts or achievements. Now because of Jesus the Kingdom of God is not about achieving anything from God, it is about freely receiving from God His righteousness, as His sons and daughters reigning with Christ in the earth. Grace crushed the enemy, Grace crushes the works of darkness, and the Good News when preached apart from the law, is the power of God working to save mankind from the ministry of condemnation and death. Grace when preached as the person of Jesus is the covenant, all through Him, crushes and pulls down every argument of religion and anything else that comes against the knowledge of God. Including our thoughts. When Jesus is in us by His Spirit He gives us the power of the gospel to take our thoughts captive to make them submitted to Jesus. We rest in Jesus and He through the power of His might crushes all that the enemy has built up in doctrines born of lies and any other thing that exalts itself against the knowledge of God. Jesus our Grace brings faith to people as we preach the gospel!

Grace causes us to live a lifestyle of repentance. The Greek word for repent "metanoia" meaning to change our mind, is what happens as we rightly believe that this life we live in Christ in us. It's He who leads us! We change our minds through out our day as the Holy Spirit reminds us of who we are in Jesus, reminding us of what Jesus has done. We can't help but to change our mind and choose Jesus. His Way, His Truth, His Life in us! The beautiful picture of the

Hebrew word for repent is “Teshuva” which has a symbolic meaning, because of the cross of Christ, return to Grace. Isn't that beautiful? The goodness of God, Jesus our Grace, has made a way in which He Himself in us, by His Spirit leads us to change our mind through out our day!

TWELVE

Grace that qualifies

RELIGION BRINGS an ideology that if you want to serve God you need to get your life together. You need to become a better you. It's an ideology that if we make enough changes, we can be a good person that God is happy with. If we do enough right it will outweigh the wrongs! If we memorize enough Bible scriptures we learn to have positive thinking. If we give enough, do enough good deeds, and attend church, mass, or temple. If we pray enough, if we go to confession if we participate in Rash Hashanah, or we get baptized, if we, if we, if you if you. And man do we try! So many of us tried and tried still. We want to be good people. We don't want God mad at us. We want our friends and family to believe we are good and that we have it together. But most importantly we want to believe that we are good. The problem is, that our own conscious condemns us. So when we don't know who we are in Jesus we are left with who we are and we know what we are. We know who we are when we are alone with our thoughts. The enemy comes and makes it worse by bringing lies and confusion. We think if we just get it together enough to go to church this Sunday it will help us be a better person.If we just read more of the Bible or say prayers scripted for particular issues of life, we will be better for it. So we fight hard to put the condemnation out of our minds, to push down the guilt and shame, and put a smile on our faces and we show up to church. We made it through the doors. The people all seem so happy and blessed. You smile and wave, shake some hands, and hug a neck or two. And for a moment you forget how shameful and guilt-ridden you were feeling on the way that morning. You see some familiar faces and life in that brief moment feels like you're good. Then the music starts and everyone else seems to be free to worship. They're lifting hands and singing. So you feel compelled to be like them, after all they seem like God is happy with them, and must be pretty spiritual if they're raising their hands and singing!. Maybe if you sing to God and lift your hands it will happen. So you push past the insecurity and manage to lift a hand and as you sing the tears come. You want it so badly you could almost break down right there and beg God to forgive you and make you into the person you want to be! The music ends though and it felt good for a moment to be vulnerable. You felt better after worship. Then the preacher gets up and preaches his message. Wouldn't you know it! He is preaching right to you. So you start to listen and he quotes some scriptures and he articulates how if you want to become all God intended you to be, you have to do x, y, and z. And he tells you how if you do these things, God will hear from heaven and answer your pleas. You make your notes! This has to be it. This has to be how you get free. So in the end, you raise your hand for the preacher to pray for you that you can live a better life and do what God told the Man of God to tell you that morning! So you leave hopeful even though truth be told you didn't understand half of what he was saying! But you have made up your mind things are going to be different from now on. You're going to implement these things in your life and it's going to get better.

Monday morning comes and you implement the new steps and you're feeling good! You have a better day at work, and even share a little with a co-worker about how you're feeling better because your pastor talked about these new things you're trying and so far it seems to be helping. Tuesday comes and then Wednesday. Life seems to be getting better. You're starting to look forward to next Sunday. But Thursday arrives and brings its own set of circumstances and you forget to implement a step or two. Your boss calls you into his office and makes you feel like trash for messing up at work, threatens your job, you get a call that a relative has passed on, or walk out to the parking lot to find someone has broken into your car and stolen valuables. You get angry and suddenly, that person you have been trying so hard not to be shows up! You say some choice words get in your car to drive home without a care. You turn the radio channel back to your favorite secular songs and just like that the thoughts come. Just like that you begin to think God doesn't hear you when you pray and the feelings of abandonment start to creep up, and you wonder if God is even around.

"See, that stuff doesn't work. You messed it up and forgot to do the step now look at you. You blew it and knew you would anyway. Forget church this Sunday, this pastor and everyone else will know you're the one loser that couldn't do it!" So you begin to come up with reasons why you can't go. Instead of spending time with Jesus you call that "old friend" because they "get you" and they always seem to understand your misery. The cycle continues and for years this has been the way. So you drag yourself to church with shame and guilt because you believe that you will never be qualified to make God happy. You believe you will never qualify for His blessings. You believe that you will never be qualified to tell people about Jesus because you can't get it right yourself.

The same could be said for attending and putting into practice a 12-step program. Which we know works, "if you keep coming"! Therapy sessions, if you pay enough for a good counselor, maybe they can help you be a better person. By the way, I'm not saying there isn't a time or place when programs and counseling aren't beneficial. It's just a cycle of trying to get good enough and the moment you stop going, it won't work anymore. You are condemned to relapse because they have all told you who you are! You are a "sinner saved by grace", you're an "addict in recovery," or you're a "normal individual having a mental health struggle".

But if you keep up the good work you will become a better version of yourself.

The problem is the moment it fails because you didn't do it right, you missed a meeting, ignored a sponsor's call, missed a counseling session, or the counseling advice just doesn't seem to change how you feel, your conscious condemns you and the cycle starts over.

Yet there is good news. Let me break this down. The preaching of how to, and if you want this you have to do this, is the way of the old covenant of law. It puts the requirement on the people to get right and do right to please God. Anything that declares God is mad at you, disappointed in you, ashamed of you is the teaching of the law. Anything or anyone who declares that God is storing up his wrath for you if you don't repent and get right with God is of the law.

Anyone who says that Jesus died for them so you have to live for Him, proving that you are worthy of the cross, is teaching law mixed with Grace. The truth is **we** will never be able to please God. That's why Jesus came and did it all for us. The Bible tells us that when the law is preached to this day, it brings a veil and puts it over the people's hearts and they cannot understand the truth! So no matter how much you want it, if the law or ways of the law are preached we cannot understand. If the law is still written on your heart, you cannot understand. Why do you think God said He will remove the heart of stone from your flesh and give you a heart of flesh? Ezekiel further wrote that God said "And I will put my Spirit within you and cause you to walk in my statutes and obey my rules. (Ezekiel 36:26-27) This was prophesying of Jesus and the new covenant to come. Since the law was not given to make us holy, following it will never make you or qualify you to be who you think you should be and we can never meet the righteous requirement of the law in our efforts to try and follow the old covenant of law. But some preachers and pastors do not understand that themselves, or worse, don't want to hear the truth because then they would have to change what they have been preaching for years. If they only realized that it's the good news of Jesus' blood and the finished work of the cross establishing a new covenant for us to live in Him, His covenant of Grace and it qualifies us all, they would preach their people free and they would begin to see miracles happening in their ministry.

We get text messages almost weekly about how the gospel of Grace set someone free in our meetings. We see and hear testimonies of people getting healed because faith came when they heard the good news. The good news can sometimes be as simple as telling someone Jesus wants to heal them. When they receive that and believe, they receive and are healed. So when the Lord called me to this mission of preaching the gospel of Grace, miracles just began to follow. If we could just get the word out, the message of Jesus bringing Grace and Truth, and that His covenant of Grace replaced the old covenant of law, we would see a massive shift in the body of Christ in our nation. This is why it is so important that we understand that armor is our identity in Christ! It is who He has made us to be in Him. And when we believe this completely when we substantiate this is what Jesus has done for us, we can live the life of His new covenant of Grace and withstand the lies of the enemy. Even when those lies come through other believers who simply can't understand the truth yet because they have been taught law and Grace mixed. We have to show them. We have to tell them and watch as they get set free. You are qualified because of Grace because there is no other way by which to be qualified!

THIRTEEN

The why Grace

HAVE you ever stopped and just thought to yourself, why has God done all this? Why is God doing all of this? An all-powerful creator who can do whatever He wants, why go through all of this time doing all He has done, what He is doing now and will do in the future? Why me? There have been sermons preached and songs written for centuries on the question of why, what's the divine goal of God in all this? The Psalmist wrote as well in Psalm 8:4, "What is man that you are mindful of him, and the son of man that you care for him?"

So I know I am not the first person to ask why God has done all this. When we look intently into the Word of God we can see God's divine purpose. We can see the ending of all of this. I don't know about you, but for me, it helps bring understanding when we know the why and how it ends.

So I want to take you on a short journey and put it all together to look at the end God has in mind for us. What is His goal? Has it all been necessary for the human race to get to what God wants and accomplish His purposes? Let's start with what is His purpose for us His creation and what is His purpose for redeeming His creation. The answers to these questions are in Romans 3:23 and Romans 8:21. Simply put the answers are the glory of God and the glory of the children of God. God's plan or purpose for man was to have a family, a creation in His very own image, and DNA. His purpose was to give man His glory. However, sin interrupted that plan and man missed God's glory. Sin, it's that word. The word that we all think of and immediately associate with God's punishment that comes when we sin. We were almost all raised, no matter what denomination of Christianity, no matter what level of Judaism, that sin is what brings the punishment of God or wrath of God on our lives. So we connect that to condemnation and the fear of hell if we don't get right with God and beg Him to forgive us our sins. There are penances and prayers devoted to achieving the forgiveness of God. But that's not how God thinks. God's thoughts now, because of the new covenant of Grace, are always of the glory man will miss if he sins. You see now because of Jesus, when we sin we give up God's glory. The good news is, we are qualified to have it again! That's what repentance is about. That's the reason for redemption through Jesus, is glory to glory to glory.

What do you mean by the glory of man? I thought only God was to be glorified. That's because the law has taught us that only God receives the glory. But before you panic and think uh-oh where's this going? Let's establish this one thing. God gets all the glory from us. He alone is worthy as far as the One who deserves. But that's why Jesus came! That's why a new covenant born from His blood was needed to fulfill the purpose of God in our lives. It was God's plan from the beginning to give us His glory! When sin detoured that, God said this is what it will take to give my children my glory. Well, pastor what is the glory of God exactly? It is the manifested presence of Himself, and the sometimes even tangible grandeur and loveliness, warmth, peace, and joy, magnified so that His character is revealed. It is the essence of all He is, and the beautiful thing is His glory is released through His Holy Spirit. So knowing that the plan was to give us His glory, we see that He planned to put Himself in us!

> "For God knew his people in advance, and he chose them to become like his Son so that his Son would be the firstborn among many brothers and sisters. And having chosen them, he called them to come to him. And having called them, he gave them right standing with himself. And having given them right standing, **he gave them his glory.**"
>
> Romans 8:29-30 NLT

It was God's objective to have a family. That His Son Jesus would be the firstborn among other sons and daughters! We don't see this when the law is preached. From the standpoint of the law, we do not deserve anything like this. That Jesus is "the **only** begotten Son...". We all know the scripture, John 3:16, it's blasted everywhere and has been the bedrock of what many and most have declared as preaching the gospel. We have heard it for decades and decades, and it is the Truth. For God did in truth, so love the world that He sent Jesus. But dying on the cross for our sins was only a part of why Jesus came. But if we knew that the law was in truth called the ministry of condemnation, then we would have caught a clue to the very next verse in John 3:17 when John wrote, "God did not send His Son into the world to condemn it, but that the world through Him might be saved." There's that word again "saved", salvation (Soteria - Greek) meaning deliverance from our enemies, all evils, sickness and disease, fear and depression... whatever attack the enemy tries to bring, Jesus has provided Deliverance through Him. Deliverance from sin. A sin that interrupted the process of God giving man His glory. So when we look at the scripture and realize God's objective, we see that God wanted Jesus to be the first of many "begotten sons and daughters". It's simple in one way, if you only have one son and you want more, you have more. Why else would God tell Adam before the fall to be fruitful and multiply? Adam was the first man, and we see that God's objective was to fill the earth with children who would be children of God, and God would give them His Spirit, and His glory, and have a family that God created. So why all the history? Sin is why the history of all God has done, has happened. He worked to redeem His children so that He might put His glory in us. So Jesus was part of the plan. Through Jesus we are justified, "and whom He justified, He also glorified." The only begotten, became the first of many. God glorified Jesus and put Him at His right hand and made Jesus the advocate of all His children. To those who have received Him. (John 1:12-13). It is the divine purpose of creation and the divine reason of redemption. God will have His children. All of this was to redeem what God had lost! In the story of the prodigal son, we often focus on the sins of the son and how he squandered away everything and then highlighted the return, the homecoming. But we miss out on the point! The Father had lost His son. In Luke 15 the lost sheep, who lost out? It was the shepherd. The lost coin, who lost out? It was the woman. The lost son, who lost out? It was the Father. It is what He exclaims at the end. "He was lost, but now he is found!" So we see that even Jesus in Luke 15 was revealing that the Father had lost His sons and daughters because of sin. So Jesus was the plan to redeem them all! We see in Romans the perspective of Jesus, referring to us as brothers and sisters. But in Hebrews, we see it from the perspective of the Father.

> "God, for whom and through whom everything was made, **chose to bring many children into glory**. And it was only right that he should make Jesus, through his suffering, a perfect leader, fit to bring them into their salvation."
>
> Hebrews 2:10 NLT

Both scriptures reveal a full-grown or mature child of God in their context. God desires children that are grown in Christ. He didn't stop at just revealing Christ on the earth as his only begotten Son, He made a way for Jesus to become the firstborn among many brothers and sisters and went further to restore His divine purpose by justifying us through Christ and then He also glorified us! He sent Jesus so that we could have Sonship! The complete expression of Jesus His Son, is God's divine plan in the many sons and daughters. He did this by justifying us and then by glorifying us. God is never going to stop short of His plans because He is faithful to complete what He started. He wanted sons and daughters and He is going to see that through until He has fulfilled His goal of exactly that. He made the way for the entirety of heaven to be filled with glorified sons and daughters, that's why He redeemed mankind. His love and desire for a family was never just going to go away because of what Adam did. God made a way through Jesus, the Second Man also called the Last Man, to redeem what He set out to do from the beginning.

How did Jesus go from the only Son to the firstborn among many? Well, Jesus told us how He was going to do it!

> "Jesus replied, "Now the time has come for the Son of Man to enter into **his glory.** I tell you the truth, unless a kernel of wheat is planted in the soil and dies, **it remains alone.** But its death **will produce many new kernels—a plentiful harvest of new lives.**"
>
> John 12:23-24 NLT

Jesus was the kernel of wheat. God chose to take His seed and put it in the ground and He died. Then resurrected as the firstborn among many. "A plentiful harvest of new lives!" Concerning His part in the Trinity, His divinity, Jesus is still the Son, now glorified next to the Father as King of kings and Lord of lords. But from the time of His resurrection onward through forever, He is our brother the King. His life is now found in us by His Spirit. Let's see that in the Word.

> "And because of his glory and excellence, he has given us great and precious promises. These are the promises **that enable you to share his**

divine nature and escape the world's corruption caused by human desires."

2 Peter 1:4 NLT

It's His divine nature in us because He is the new covenant scripted from His blood and all that the finished work of the cross has given us in these precious promises that allow us to be as He is. (1 John 4:17). That divine nature in us, is received by our complete faith in Jesus as we surrender our lives moment to moment to the leading of His Spirit. I am His and He is mine! He lives in me and I live through Him. He alone has brought this abundant life to us as a gift! It's unmerited, underserved, it's Grace. We have received the spirit of adoption through Him by which from within us we declare "Father, I will obey" (Romans 8:15-16). We see the word Abba used in this scripture, but the Hebrew word Abba, literally means "Father I will obey". They still use this word today in their culture with raising their children. When a father corrects his child or has a time of teaching his children, they address him as Abba, because it is a word whose context brings with it a deep respect out of love and because of who he is to them relationally. It's similar to our American word Daddy, when used in the context from a child who loves and cries out "Daddy" from a place of excitement or desperation. So when we receive Jesus into our lives the Spirit in us produces Abba in us, more and more and we cry out to Him and address Him from a place of love for Him and reverence, respect, and awe of our Father. This is how we also know we have become a son or daughter. The Spirit of God in us, the full expression of the Son of God in us by His Spirit produces this love in us for the Father and others. God is love. It makes perfect sense, that when He is truly in us, He would produce love in us. That's what Grace has done for us and in us. Grace produces love, Grace produces holiness, and Grace produces obedience. Jesus is Grace in us. This is what satisfies the heart of the Father, because of what Jesus has done, the Father now has many sons and daughters. Jesus again clues us in on when this moment in time took place.

> "Don't cling to me," Jesus said, "for I haven't yet ascended to the Father. But go **find my brothers** and tell them, 'I am ascending to my Father and **your Father**, to my God and **your God**."
>
> John 20:17 NLT

Jesus had become the eldest Son because His death and resurrection had redeemed us. Now as many as will receive Him God has given them the place of sons and daughters. Jesus knew this and told Mary to go find His brothers and tell them He was going to His Father and their Father. Jesus knew what had happened and that all He had been sent to do and accomplish had been for that moment. It is finished. We are now part of the family of God for those who receive Jesus. The Father's desire is for sons and daughters to be jointheirs with Jesus in glory. Again, the Father's ultimate goal is to have a family of many sons and daughters to share His glory in. How did God bring this about? How can He do this? Let's look at the Word again.

> "God, for whom and through whom everything was made, chose to bring **many children into**

> **glory.** And it was only right that he should make Jesus, through his suffering, **a perfect leader, fit to bring them into their salvation.** So now Jesus and the ones he makes holy have the same Father. That is why Jesus is not ashamed to call them **His brothers and sisters.**"
>
> Hebrews 2:10-11 NLT

We see the One who is the perfect leader that brings salvation and we see the ones that He came for to set apart to the Father, and we see they have the same Father. We see they are one in Jesus and the Father. The amazing thing about this is we saw Jesus talking to the Father about this very thing before He went to the cross. He told the Father in John 17 that He was praying for all of us that we would all be one like He and the Father are One and that we would all be One in Him and the Father. So Jesus revealed His heart, which was the Father's heart as well because they are One, and now that unification is available to all that receive Jesus and His new covenant of Grace. As we look more and more into the Word of God we know that Jesus as a man was given life from God. He was conceived by the Holy Spirit in a virgin girl named Mary (Matthew 1:20). So the DNA of Jesus is of God and not of this world. Likewise, when we are born again into Christ, we are born of the Spirit of God (John 1:13; 3:5). Therefore we are all of the One. One important part to know in this is when we see the word "of" in Greek, it is "out of". So that puts it into proper perspective. We are NOT God, we are OF God in Christ. We are His offspring by the Spirit, sons and daughters born out of God. The life which God has in heaven, the life and His glory He has imparted to us by His Spirit.

Grace and Truth came through Jesus, the very essence of who He is to abide in us. So when the Bible says we are "saved by Grace through faith in Jesus", it is saying we are saved, delivered from the law of sin and death by Jesus our new covenant from His blood, Grace, by putting our faith in Jesus substantiating that He is all of this and more. He is the Way, the Truth, and the Life. All in Him, united by Him through His Holy Spirit with the Father, having become children born again out of God. Notice that nowhere in any of that do we find the question of sin anymore. It just goes away, having no place in the new covenant of Jesus. Sin came through Adam, and even though it has been dealt with and judged at the cross on Jesus' body, it can still present itself in our flesh and have to be dealt with as it should, and in that, we are only returned to the point Adam was. But the beautiful thing is because of the redemption of Jesus, access to the Tree of Life has been restored making us partakers of the very life of God Himself, so sin has no power over us, so when it does present itself, and we know who we are in Jesus, One with the Father through the Spirit of God, we have the authority and ability to choose Grace over and over again. Sin is defeated and we are children of God.

The great divine purpose and goal of the Father to have sons and daughters that He put His glory into has been realized. All that we are as His children, is because of Jesus, because the Father desired and loved us so much that He sent Jesus to do what we could not do for ourselves. Through His new covenant of Grace, we are united with Jesus through the Spirit of God and have become His own. He is glorified and we have received His glory. When people see us, our lives should reveal the glory of our Father who is in us, His name is Jesus!

So now we know the why. It seems like the explanation is a lot, but the simplicity of it is that God's divine purpose and plan was to have a family. When sin thwarted that, God made a way through His only begotten Son, to come and overthrow the power of sin by fulfilling the righteous requirement of the old covenant of law and putting it away, to establish a new covenant in His blood. A covenant of Grace in which we have been redeemed, justified, and glorified in Jesus! I don't know about you, but for me, knowing the why has only brought me to a place of wanting more of God. To know Him more, to talk about Him more, to preach the good news of this covenant of Grace, a covenant that is Jesus Himself.

When my wife and I talk to people about this, one of the things we constantly recognize that begins to happen as they realize what Jesus has done, is faith comes to them, or grows more in them. You can see it in their countenance and really in their eyes. My wife and I just went out for a New Year's Eve dinner together at a new restaurant in town. We thought we would just get away for the evening and be together. When we walked in, we were greeted by a waitress. For this book, we will call her Aria. We have known Aria for almost a year. She had been a waitress at another restaurant my wife and I and friends would often go to after church. We had talked to her about the Lord several times over that year. But there she was at the new restaurant. We greeted her and requested her as our waitress. She is a great waitress and took great care of us as clientele. My wife was talking to her towards the end of the meal and asking how she was doing in college and her career path. Suddenly she says, "Okay I do want to ask y'all a question as pastors!" She went on to tell us first how she had been struggling recently with the fear of dying. She asked "How do I know for sure where I go if I die? I mean I believe in Jesus and God and I know Jesus is the son of God and He died for me, but I have just like been afraid of or scared like will I go to heaven." We shared the gospel with Her, the good news of what Jesus has done for her to assure her that all it takes to make it to heaven is for her to surrender her life to Jesus by putting her faith completely in Jesus. We talked about how Jesus has given her a gift of His Righteousness and that she is now a daughter of God. She is her Father's daughter! In just a few moments you could see faith was coming. She was hearing about the words of Jesus and all that Grace has accomplished for her and who she is now in Him and fear began to be pushed out! When she heard how much He loved her and as she trusted in the Lord that perfect Love cast out all fear, and you could see the change. She is just one of many to whom the Lord has given us the privilege of revealing His glory. When we are fully in, Jesus will bring them to you! You can't help but tell them.

So as we come to the end of volume one, and now know why God sent Jesus to establish a new covenant, I want you to know that the new covenant of Grace, the good news of Grace and Truth coming has changed everything. Anyone who tries to put you under law by preaching a different gospel than what Paul preached, is trying to "bewitch you" as the Pharisees did to the church of Galatia, mixing the law with Grace. But when we surrender fully, completely, and continuously to Jesus, His Grace produces holiness in our lives, it produces obedience in us, and qualifies us. We love others with His love and we have this confidence and boldness because we believe and know that we are qualified, having become sons and daughters of God, co-heirs with Christ! All of this because Jesus, He is... Grace and Truth that came. Now it is no longer I that lives, but Christ that lives in me, and the life I now live in the flesh I live through the Son of God. Qualified, Sanctified, Justified, and glorified as His Righteousness. Don't continue to settle for even a little leaven (old law) ruining the batch! Don't settle for an old wineskin with new wine in it. It will rupture and ruin them both! Fix your eyes on Jesus and know who you are in Him!

"For the **Grace** of God has **appeared**, bringing salvation [soteriá - deliverance] for all people, **training us** to renounce ungodliness and worldly passions, and **to live** self-controlled, upright, and **Godly lives** in the present age."

Titus 2:11-12 ESV

Connect with Us

Stay Connected with Us! Visit our church's website at www.life180.tv for more inspiring content, events, and community updates. To schedule Pastors Aaron and Cyndi Kincaid for ministry events, please call 903-844-8066 or email us at ministry@life180.tv. We'd love to continue this journey with you. See you online!

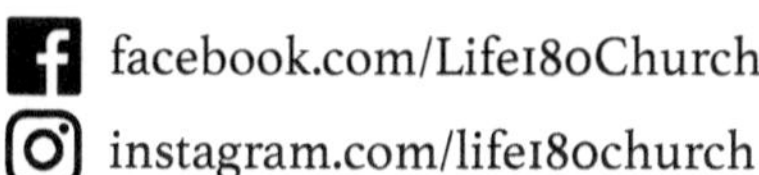

www.ingramcontent.com/pod-product-compliance
Lightning Source LLC
LaVergne TN
LVHW010107170826
845678LV00012B/2286

* 9 7 8 9 6 5 5 7 8 9 1 6 4 *